WHAT WIL ~~HAPPEN NEXT?~~
A Chronological Study of the
Book of Revelation

Content from the teaching of
JIM JOHNSON
Written and compiled by
ELISE JOHNSON

A JUSTAPREACHER MINISTRIES PUBLICATION
Satellite Beach, FL
www.justapreacherministries.org

©2021 by Jim Johnson, Elise Johnson,
and Justapreacher Ministries, Inc.
1st Edition Published 2021

**What Will Happen Next: A Chronological Study
of the Book of Revelation**
ISBN: 978-0-9860509-4-7

Cover design and layout by
Chris and Allison Wilson, Elise Johnson, and
Justapreacher Ministries
Satellite Beach, FL

Printed by Snowfall Press
1832 Woodmoor Drive, Suite 207
Monument, Colorado 80132

Chronological Order of End Time Events

This is the order of end time events that I believe the Bible has revealed. However, many of these events will happen simultaneously. I have broken the events into smaller sections to indicate which events will occur in close succession. As you read this book, keep in mind that the exact order of events is not as important as the fact that all these things <u>must</u> happen.

- Tribulation:
    - Beginning—
        - The Antichrist signs a treaty with Israel and many other nations
    - First half—
        - The sealing of the 144,000
        - The two witnesses begin their ministry
        - The first six seals
    - Midpoint—
        - The Abomination of Desolation
        - The death and resurrection of the two witnesses
        - Israel flees to the wilderness
        - The Battle of Gog and Magog begins—culminating in the Battle of Armageddon

- o Second half—
  - The Antichrist and the False Prophet administer the Mark of the Beast
  - The seventh seal
  - The trumpet judgments
  - The bowl judgments

- o End—
  - The destruction of Babylon
  - The Second Coming
  - The Battle of Armageddon

- Millennial Kingdom:
  - o Jesus steps onto the Mount of Olives
  - o Old Testament and Tribulation saints receive new bodies
  - o The Marriage Supper of the Lamb—lasts the entire Millennial Kingdom

- Post Millennial Kingdom:
  - o The Final Rebellion
  - o The Great White Throne Judgment
  - o The New Heaven and New Earth—lasts for eternity

Table of Contents

Authorization

This book has been compiled by my daughter Elise Johnson from the years of my teaching on the book of Revelation. I have been very involved in the process throughout, but I am extremely grateful to her and to the Lord for her God-given gifts of writing and editing. She has done a marvelous job, and I couldn't be prouder of her! This book wouldn't be here at this time and in this form without her! It has my full approval.

Jim Johnson

Preface

Jesus is coming soon. As we near the end of the time period of the Church Age, world events continue to align in ways that signal the end. Because we need to be looking towards what comes next (Philippians 3:13-15, Revelation 1:3), this book will study the prophetic events of Revelation chronologically. We will use Revelation 1:1-3 as a jumping off point, then move into chapter four. Chapter four contains the first of John's visions of what must take place after the Church Age ends. This book will not cover chapters two and three, because they contain messages for the Church during the Church Age, whereas this book will focus mostly on the events following the Church Age.

The book of Revelation is the result of John recording exactly what Jesus told him to, in three parts (Revelation 1:19). His vision of Jesus and the lampstands on the Isle of Patmos is the first part (Chapter 1), admonishments for our current time (the Church Age) come next (Chapters 2-3), and what is to come after the Church Age was recorded last (Chapters 4-22). We will focus on John's visions of what is to come after the Church Age, which begin in chapter four of Revelation. John recorded the visions that Jesus gave to him, but Jesus is the true author of Revelation. Jesus inspired these prophecies.

Some might ask why we should study what comes after the Church Age since we believers will not be here for it. The answer is simple: Jesus gave this whole book as a message for the churches (Revelation 22:16), for us to learn from and pass on to others. Just as we benefit from Daniel, Isaiah, Jeremiah, and other prophets that testified concerning things that would not happen in their lifetime (1 Peter 1:10-12), our prayer is that those in the future will benefit from our study of Revelation. We must study and share what will take place next and pray that those who hear it will combine this information with faith in Jesus Christ.

The events of Revelation, like much prophecy, were not always recorded in the order that they will happen. As we study these events chronologically, don't get confused if we skip from chapter six to chapter twelve or from thirteen to eight. I developed the order of events we will use in this book through intense study with my friend Dr. Tony Kessinger,[1] and it does require studying the chapters in a different order than they were originally compiled. This is often how prophecy must be studied, and so we treat Revelation the same way, because it is prophecy (Revelation 1:3; 22:7, 18-19).

I have been studying Revelation for many years, and I have such a passion for it. I can't wait to show you what I believe God has shown me over decades of study. I do not take the responsibility of teaching the Word lightly (James 3:1). I have wrestled with and studied everything laid out in this book thoroughly. I charge you, however, to examine the scripture for yourself to verify what I have to say. As you come upon scriptures referenced in this book, please take time to read them alongside the text. Unless otherwise noted, the version I will be using for scripture references in this book is the English Standard Version. God's inspired Word illuminates the truths in this book much better than I ever could. Studying Revelation is so rewarding if you take it chronologically and literally, so let's dive in!

---

[1] Please also read and examine for yourself Tony's book, *Things That Must Take Place*. You can find the full reference for that book in this book's bibliography.

Introduction
Revelation 1:1-3

John recorded the book of Revelation while imprisoned on the Isle of Patmos in A.D. 96. At that time, the Roman Empire was under Domitian's rule.[2] Jesus appeared to John on the Isle of Patmos, and John recorded exactly what Jesus told him to. In fact, at one point in Revelation, John begins to write down a vision, and Jesus won't let him (Revelation 10:4). Jesus decided exactly what is in this book. While John put the Book of Revelation on paper, Jesus is really the one who wrote it. This truly is "the revelation of *Jesus Christ*, which God gave Him to show to His servants the things that must soon take place" (Revelation 1:1). This message is for us, who are living right now in the Church Age, and it is also for those who will come to faith during the seven-year Tribulation period that we will learn about in this study.

There are two particularly important words in that first verse of Revelation. These are things that "<u>must soon</u> take place." Let's look closely at the implication of these words. We will begin with 'must.' Jesus states that the events recorded in Revelation *must* take place three separate times in this book (Revelation 1:1, 4:1, 22:6). This book is not apocalyptic writing, as some say. If Jesus said that these things *must* take place, they are not debatable. They are literal prophecies, and they *must* be taken as such.

Sometimes people assume that the events chronicled in Revelation are symbolic. That is not the case. There is a lot of symbolic language in the Bible, but when symbols are used, the scripture consistently explains what each symbol represents. For example, in this first chapter of Revelation, Jesus is

---

[2]MacArthur, John. *The MacArthur Bible Commentary*. Thomas Nelson, 2005.

depicted standing amongst seven golden lampstands and holding seven stars (Revelation 1:12-16). This beautiful symbolic language could be confusing, but God doesn't leave us to wonder what it means. Just a few verses later, He explains that the stars represent angels of the churches, and the lampstands are representative of the churches themselves (Revelation 1:20).

We see this approach throughout the Bible. If the Bible uses symbolism, it tells us what is being symbolized (1 Corinthians 10:1-4, John 7:37-39, Ezekiel 37:1-11, Zechariah 5:5-8). We could talk about many other examples, but I won't belabor the point. God wants us to understand His teaching, so unless He says something is symbolic, we must assume it's literal. Jesus said that these things must take place. That means that we can interpret them literally, and as we interpret the scriptures literally, they come alive.

Now that we understand that these end time events are guaranteed, let's study that word 'soon' from verse one. It has been nearly two thousand years since John wrote this prophecy down, so what does God mean by 'soon?' In our earthly minds, 'soon' should've already happened. To help answer this question, let's refer to the original text. John originally penned Revelation in Greek. 'Soon' in this verse is translated from the Greek word 'en taxeii.'[3] The literal translation of 'en taxeii' is 'quickly,' or 'speedily.' It is the word that our English word 'tachometer' is derived from. A tachometer doesn't measure the amount of time until something happens. It measures the speed at which it happens. This word was translated in most modern versions of the Bible as 'soon,' but a better translation would be 'quickly.' Once the things recorded in Revelation begin

---

[3] Strong, James. Strong's Exhaustive Concordance of the Bible. Abingdon Press, 1890. Print.

happening, they will progress in rapid succession. They will take place quickly.

Now we understand that the things detailed in this book must happen, and that when they begin to happen, they will happen quickly. However, verse three of Revelation also says that "the time is near" for these prophecies to be fulfilled. How can this be true if it has been nearly two thousand years since John recorded these prophecies? God does not count time the same way that we do. The time is described as 'near' because these events are the next thing on Jesus' timeline. God has not told us how long the Church Age will be, but when it is over, the events recorded in Revelation (beginning with the Tribulation) will commence. John recorded the things that are, i.e., the Church Age, and the things that are to take place after the Church Age ends, i.e., the Tribulation and subsequent ages, according to Jesus' instruction (Revelation 1:19).

So far, there have been four separate 'ages' of God's work in the world. God works in different ways in different time periods (Hebrews 1:1-2), but His message always stays the same. No matter the era, salvation is and always has been by faith in God alone, in His Word and His provision for man's sin. We know now that God's provision comes (and has always come) through His son Jesus. God offers this gift of salvation through Jesus' sinless life, death, and resurrection, and we must receive it by faith alone. When people receive this salvation now, they become part of God's Church (Matthew 16:15-18). We are currently in the Church Age, but three ages have come before this one. Here is a breakdown of these ages:

1. The Garden—This age stretched from Creation until the Fall. At that time, sin did not exist for humans. They had total unity with God. The first sin triggered a new age.
2. The Age of Conscience—This age was in effect from Adam until Moses. Humans were sinful and separated

6

from God because of the Fall, but God had not given humanity the Law yet. Their sin was different than Adam's, because his sin came about through direct disobedience to a command of God. They did not have commands of God to disobey, but death was the evidence and consequence of their sin (Romans 5:12-14).

3. The Age of Law—This age began when God gave Moses the Ten Commandments. These were commands of God that the people were supposed to obey. The Israelites tried to adhere to them, but God knew that they wouldn't be able to keep the Law perfectly, so He laid out rules within the Law that allowed their sin to be temporarily covered by animal sacrifice. God gave the Law to man to reveal man's inability to keep God's Law (Romans 3:20). The Law didn't create sin. It just illuminates the sin that is already in people, like an MRI illuminates sickness. The Law shows people their sin so that they recognize their need for God. One sin condemns you (James 2:10), but people don't seem to believe that. Many people believe that you can get to heaven if you are 'good enough,' i.e., if you don't sin too much. God wants people to sin enough that they will recognize their need for His forgiveness (Romans 5:20-21). This stage prepared people for the next age.

4. The Age of Grace (the Church Age)—This age began at Pentecost, when God's Spirit came to indwell believers who received Jesus' cleansing by faith (Acts 2:1-21). After God's people had a chance to recognize their need for grace while they were under the Law, God sent His Son Jesus to be the final sacrifice for our sins. We do not need an animal to temporarily cover our sins any longer, because Jesus died once and for all

as the perfect sacrifice for our sins. He is the Lamb of God who takes away the sins of the world (John 1:29). After He was crucified, He rose again to defeat the death that has reigned over mankind since the Fall. All those who respond by faith to Jesus receive the seal of the indwelling Holy Spirit (Ephesians 1:13-14), and they become one with Jesus and part of His Church (Ephesians 1:22-23). The Church Age will end right before the Tribulation, when Jesus returns to call His Church home to heaven (Revelation 3:10, 1 Thessalonians 1:9-10, 1 Thessalonians 4:13-18). This is called the Rapture.

The Bible teaches that there are three ages yet to come. These are the time periods that we will study in this book, and they are as follows:

5. The Tribulation—This seven-year period will begin soon after the Rapture of the Church. It is what comes next. John begins describing this age in chapter four of the book of Revelation. This time period is referenced in many other places in the Bible (Daniel 9:27, Matthew 24:3-31, Jeremiah 30:4-7).

6. The Millennial Kingdom (the Messianic Kingdom)— This age is the thousand-year reign of Jesus Christ physically on the earth. During this time there will still be sin, but it will be lessened, and there will also still be salvation. Jesus will reign over the earth in peace and prosperity. The end of this period will be marked by a final war and judgment (Revelation 20:1-10, Isaiah 65:18-25, Jeremiah 30:18-31:14).

7. The New Heaven and New Earth—At that final war and judgment, Jesus will be victorious against Satan and will cast him into the Lake of Fire forever. Then the current earth and heavens will pass away, and Jesus will

rebuild a new heaven and earth as His eternal kingdom. This is the final age, because it will endure forever, and there will be no more death or pain. All who place their faith and trust in Jesus will live in God's presence forever, glorifying Him for eternity (Revelation 21:1-4, Isaiah 65:17).

We are to study all these things so that we will be ready for Jesus' return, and so that we will receive reward when He does (Revelation 1:3; 22:6-7, 10-13). Satan has convinced many in the Church to fear the book of Revelation. There are many different interpretations of it, and because of that, many pastors are afraid to teach it. This is a tragedy, because it is the only book in the Bible that promises blessing to those who study it and take it to heart (Revelation 1:3). Through this study, my prayer is that God will lift away the fear and show us how easy this book is to understand.

Why should we believe anything written in this book? The last chapter of Revelation says it best: "These words are trustworthy and true" (Revelation 22:6). The Bible is the Word of God itself, and it is an incredible document. It is the most reliably translated manuscript in the world, with more original copies than any other classic work.[4] The book of Revelation itself is a beautiful reflection of the rest of the Bible. Around three-quarters of the prophecy in Revelation echoes passages elsewhere in the Bible. There is no way that Revelation could have just been written by John and tacked onto the Bible at the last minute. Jesus took Old Testament prophecies, reiterated them, and compiled them in a way that would help us understand their true meaning. Jesus also provided new insight

---

[4] Strobel, Lee. *The Case for Christ: A Journalist's Personal Investigation of the Evidence for Jesus.* Zondervan, 2016.

through His words that John penned. No matter how helpless we may feel in this world, remember that God knows what will happen at every moment from here to eternity, and He has given us prophecy that illuminates what is coming next. Things in the world will continue to get worse as we near the end (2 Timothy 3:1-5). As this happens, take it as a reminder that Jesus is coming soon, and let this be a comfort: everything is right on schedule.

Chapter One
The Presence of God
Revelation 4

•••

The Identity of the Twenty-Four Elders
Revelation 4:1-4

In John's first vision of what is to come after the Church Age, he sees God the Father in heaven, seated on a throne and surrounded by a rainbow. His throne is surrounded by twenty-four elders, seated on their own thrones. John was not the first person to record a vision of heaven in the Bible. Isaiah and Ezekiel have also described encounters with heaven (Isaiah 6:1-7, Ezekiel 1:1-28), and their accounts bear a striking resemblance to John's vision. Ezekiel's account even describes the same rainbow glory that John saw around the throne. That rainbow is a guarantee and representation of God's glory and faithfulness (Genesis 9:8-17).

There are lots of similarities between the three accounts of heaven, but John's vision includes something that Isaiah and Ezekiel's didn't. The Old Testament prophets did not see the thrones of the twenty-four elders in their visions. Why would these be missing from Old Testament visions of heaven? I believe it is because John saw a future heaven, at a time when the Church has been caught up to God and is reigning with Him. Isaiah and Ezekiel did not see the elders because they saw the heaven of their time, and at that time no saints were ruling with God. I believe the Bible teaches that the elders John saw in his vision represent the Church, raptured to heaven before the Tribulation. Scripture teaches that the true Church will rule and reign with Jesus (Revelation 2:26-29, 3:21-22, 2 Timothy

2:10-12). The elders in this passage do not represent the angels, Old Testament saints, or Tribulation saints.

As John is describing what he sees in heaven, he uses comparisons for the things he is unable to fully comprehend ("had the appearance of jasper and carnelian" Revelation 4:3), but he describes the elders very clearly, as if he recognizes them. He deals the same way with the four living creatures described in the next passage (Revelation 4:6-8). He does this because the four living creatures have been written about before; Ezekiel saw them in his vision of heaven and described them thoroughly (Ezekiel 1:5-14). In the same way, John describes the elders as if he is already familiar with them. We should be familiar with them too because they have been written about before. The white robes of the elders are a clue to their identity.

Jesus told John that those who obtain righteousness through faith will walk with Him in white (Revelation 3:4-6). These elders on the thrones are those who conquer, walk with Jesus, and are clothed in white. Although white robes are not specific to the Church alone (Revelation 6:9-11, 7:13-14), the Church is one of the groups that will be clothed in white. Let's look at some other attributes of these elders and explain why they specifically point to the Church.

In addition to their white robes, the elders are wearing crowns. There are a few different words for crown in the original Greek that all have different connotations. The word used in this passage is 'stephanos,' which denotes a crown given as a reward, something you earn; 'spoils of the victor,' if you will.[5] God promises to give crowns to those who are faithful to believe even through trials (Revelation 2:10, 3:11-13; 2 Timothy

---

[5] Strong, James. Strong's Exhaustive Concordance of the Bible. Abingdon Press, 1890. Print.

4:6-8). All along, God's people have been promised crowns, and when John had a vision of what will be after the church age, believers were there with their crowns, reigning with God. The elders are not angels. Angels are ministering servants, and they do not reign. They do not receive crowns and they are not redeemed as sons like we are (Hebrews 1:3-7, 13-14). But of all the believers throughout history that will receive crowns, who will be able to physically reign in heaven at this time?

John's vision of the elders occurs before the Lamb begins opening the seals that bring judgment in the Tribulation (Revelation 5:1-10), so this vision depicts heaven prior to the beginning of the Tribulation. Who, of all the Saints, will receive physical bodies, be robed in white, and dwell in heaven with God before the Tribulation? The answer is only the Church (Revelation 3:10, 1 Thessalonians 1:9-10, 1 Thessalonians 4:13-18, 1 Corinthians 15:51-55). The Old Testament saints are dwelling with God right now (Matthew 17:1-8, John 8:56-58), but they will not receive new physical bodies until the end of the Tribulation (Daniel 12:1-3, 13; John 5:28-29). Likewise, the Tribulation saints (those who come to believe in Jesus, do not accept the mark of the beast, and/or are martyred during the Tribulation) will also receive new bodies at the end of the Tribulation period (Revelation 6:9-11, 20:4-6). Both groups of saints will get a chance to rule with Christ during the Millennial Kingdom, but the elders in this passage are the only group that will be redeemed both spiritually and physically before the Tribulation. The elders are the Church.

The Church is represented in this vision by twenty-four elders for a specific reason. Some believe that the number twenty-four represents the twelve tribes of Israel and the twelve Apostles together, because both groups are represented in the New Jerusalem (Revelation 21:9-14). However, these two passages are not necessarily related. There is no scriptural reason to believe that the number twenty-four represents the

Old Testament saints and the Church combined. The number does, however, reflect the divisions of spiritual government and worship leadership that God put in place in ancient Israel. In the Old Testament, God anointed the Levites to serve as priests for the nation of Israel. He then divided the Levites into twenty-four groups, to represent the Levites as a whole (1 Chronicles 24:7-19). These divisions took turns serving and performing their duties in the temple, and the Jews followed these procedures even in Jesus' day (Luke 1:8-9). God also divided the worship leaders of the Israelites into twenty-four sections (1 Chronicles 25:1, 9-31). Just like the priests, these twenty-four sections represented the whole group of worship leaders, and they all took turns serving. In our passage, the Church is represented by twenty-four elders that are taking their turn serving with God. Since the elders' service follows the pattern of the priests and worship leaders, I believe every single member of the Church will take a turn ruling as one of the elders!

It is an amazing promise that the Church will reign with God, but we need to be ready for that day. The Rapture could happen at any moment, becoming more likely as we get further along in the last days. Jesus warns the Church to be ready (Revelation 3:14-22). There are those who attend church who are not truly sealed by the Holy Spirit, and Jesus wants those people to come to know Him. If He is not in you, you will be spit out. If you think you don't need Jesus, you will find yourself to be wretched, pitiful, poor, blind, and naked. You will be lost.

The only way you can be one of the elders and rule with Jesus is if you find true salvation. The good news is, He offers Himself to all of us! Believe in Jesus by faith and allow Him to effect real change in your life. Make sure that Christ is in you (2 Corinthians 13:5). Church membership means nothing if Jesus hasn't sealed you with His Spirit (John 2:23-25, Mark 4:1-20,

Ephesians 1:13-14). Has God revealed to you that you're lost? If so, humble yourself and believe in Jesus. He is God. He has covered your sin by His death and resurrection, and He offers you salvation. All you must do is accept Him as your Lord and Savior. He wants to seal you forever as His. Don't put it off any longer—the time for His return is near.

When we join Jesus in the air, I believe we will all have an opportunity to sit on one of those twenty-four thrones. Just as the worship leaders and priests took turns serving in the temple, we will do the same. That means that one of us could be the elder who announces Jesus' ability to open the scroll (Revelation 5:5)! It could even be you, so prepare for this possibility by telling people about Jesus' power to save and redeem all His creation.

●●●

God's Glory Seen in the Four Living Creatures
Revelation 4:5-11

In this passage, John continues to describe what he saw in the presence of God. The rumbling, flashes of lightning, and thunder coming from the throne of God call to mind God's appearance to Moses on Mount Sinai (Exodus 19:16-20). From age to age, God does not change. He was holy then, He is holy now, and He will be holy in the future. His holiness is power and might, and it appears as a storm, making Him unapproachable unless God declares you righteous. You cannot achieve righteousness on your own; it is a gift that God gives to those who place their faith in Him (Romans 4:5, 5:1-2). Throughout every time period, salvation has been by faith alone in God's power and provision for sin. Moses and Aaron were allowed on the mountain with God because God had declared them righteous, and John was taken into the presence of God because he had also been declared righteous. Just like those men, those of us who have put our faith in Jesus Christ have received righteousness from God, and we have been made able to go into the presence of God. We, like John, are welcome in His sight! Yet, because God is unchanging and eternally holy, His presence is still fearsome.

In the throne room, John saw seven torches of fire that represent the seven spirits of God. God is one being, and He never changes. So why are there seven different spirits of God? We find the answer if we study this question through the lens of the whole Bible. God has told us what these seven spirits are before. They are the Spirit of the Lord, wisdom, understanding, counsel, might, knowledge, and fear of the Lord (Isaiah 11:1-5). They are not different from God; they are facets of His deity. God uses the number seven repeatedly in scripture to represent completion and perfection. Isaiah made it clear that the perfection of God would exist in the Messiah. Jesus is the Messiah, and He is Almighty God (Isaiah 9:6-7).

Next, John described four living creatures around the throne that look like those described in Ezekiel's account of heaven (Ezekiel 1:4-14). In his vision, Ezekiel realized that the creatures were cherubim (Ezekiel 10:20-22). Cherubim are a different class of angel than seraphim. Seraphim and cherubim have separate roles. Seraphim deal with the holiness of God. Their duty is to preserve it (Isaiah 6:1-7). The cherubim have two roles: guardianship and judgment. The Bible shows them performing their guard duties when Adam and Eve were kicked out of the garden. Cherubim were posted outside the Garden of Eden to prevent man from eating from the tree of life (Genesis 3:22-24). Elsewhere in scripture, they are represented guarding the Ark of the Covenant and the Holy of Holies (1 Kings 8:6-7, Exodus 26:31-35). God designed cherubim to protect His glory. The other responsibility of the cherubim is judgement (Ezekiel 10:1-8), and we see that enacted in

Revelation. When Jesus opens the first four seals of judgment, the cherubim declare the arrival of the four horsemen (Revelation 6:1-7), and one hands out God's wrath to the seven angels bearing the seven plagues (Revelation 15:7).

John and Ezekiel's accounts describe the same creatures, but there are a couple surface level discrepancies between them. Ezekiel saw four wings on each creature, while John saw six. Both accounts describe the same four likenesses: lion, ox, human, and eagle, but Ezekiel saw four faces on each creature, while John saw one face on each creature. Finally, John saw the creatures around the throne, while Ezekiel saw them beneath the throne.

It would be easy to produce reasons why the descriptions of the cherubim differ slightly between Ezekiel and John's accounts, but any theory is just a guess. The scriptures do not reveal a clear answer. It is enough to know that there *is* an answer. God knows it, so we don't have to know it right now. Don't let these apparent differences distract you from the message of this passage and the glory of God.

The message you should not miss from this passage is this: the four living creatures are a continual manifestation of the glory of God's creation. They glorify God eternally in His presence (Revelation 4:8). That's why they have the appearance of man, lion, ox, and eagle. They represent the diversity of His creation: humanity, wild animals, domesticated animals, and birds of the sky. God uses His creation as one of the key ways that He reveals Himself to all mankind. Whenever the cherubim, as representatives of creation, give glory to God, the elders worship God in turn because of the glory of His creation (Revelation 4:9-11).

The Bible does not try to prove the existence of God. It simply states that He is (Genesis 1:1). God does not owe us proof. He is content to simply show Himself in His creation. Since the beginning, men have had evidence of God revealed to them in nature's intelligent design and have had no excuse not to believe (Romans 1:18-21). God uses His creation to accomplish many things. He uses creation to teach His children how to trust God (Matthew 6:25-32). He uses creation as proof of His omnipotence (Job 38). The only necessary proof of God's existence is in creation (Psalm 19:1-4). The heavens declare the glory of God! God doesn't need us to proclaim His glory. If humans fail to declare His name, even the rocks will cry out (Luke 19:37-40). The cherubim seen in this passage are a physical manifestation of God's glory as presented by creation. They stir the elders (that is, the Church!) to worship God and glorify Him, and when we worship God, we fulfill the purpose for which He created us. God doesn't need us to declare His glory, but He wants us to!

John knew Jesus very well—he was 'the disciple that Jesus loved.' Yet when John saw Jesus on the Isle of Patmos, he fell at His feet as though dead (Revelation 1:17-18). John's immediate response to seeing Jesus was fear and worship. As the seven torches that we learned about indicate, Jesus is God, and He is awe-inspiring. As we get to know Him, we slowly realize how little we know about Him. We will spend eternity learning more about Him and we will never run out of things to learn. His wonder and majesty can never be fully known. As C.S. Lewis so aptly put it, "every year you grow, you will find [Him] bigger."[6] We can't know everything about Him, but He offers everyone an opportunity to know Him intimately. You cannot know every detail of His character, but He wants you to know His nature. There *are* answers to the things we don't understand, and it's going to be so much fun to figure some (but not all!) of them out. Be okay with not knowing every answer.

---

[6] Lewis, Clive S. "Chapter 10: The Return of the Lion." Prince Caspian, Harper Collins, 1951, pp. 141–141.

The scripture doesn't tell us why Ezekiel saw cherubim with four wings and John saw cherubim that had six, but we know they saw the same creatures. If any human claims to have all the answers to these types of questions, run from them. Jesus is the only one who knows everything. When you study the Bible, remember that "I don't know" is a valid answer. If you are honest when you don't have the answer, you will be more credible when you say that you do. The only things we can know for sure come through scripture and the Holy Spirit. We will never figure God out completely (Romans 11:33-34). He only reveals to us what we need to know and what He wants us to know (Deuteronomy 29:29). Our responsibility is to keep seeking Him (Proverbs 25:2). We won't ever figure God out, but we can know Him (John 17:3). Have you been declared righteous, sealed by the Holy Spirit, and welcomed into God's presence? This is the crux of the issue: Do you know Jesus?

Chapter Two
The Scroll of the Title Deed
of the Earth
Revelation 5

The scroll in this passage is very important. When John thought that there was no one to open it, he despaired. There is a reason John reacted that way. Thankfully for all of us, there is someone who can open the scroll: the spotless Lamb who takes away the sin of the world.

I hope it's clear that the Lamb is Jesus. Throughout the Bible, there have been prophecies of a sacrificial lamb who takes away the sins of the world, and Jesus came to be that Lamb (John 1:29-34). When Jesus as the Lamb of God takes the scroll from the hand of the Father, every being in heaven and on earth, both the righteous and unrighteous, breaks into praise (Revelation 5:13). This is another proof that this Lamb is Jesus—no one else is to be worshipped like this. When you understand what this scroll is, you too should worship Jesus for His ability to break the seals.

Why is it so important that Jesus be able to open this scroll? The answer lies in what the scroll represents. The fall of man brought death upon the earth in three stages (Genesis 3:17-19, 1 Corinthians 15:21-22). God made the earth for Himself, but He gave temporary dominion over the earth to humanity (Genesis 1:26-28). We lost it to Satan when Adam and Eve succumbed to temptation and disobeyed God. The sinful fall of man caused death to enter the world in three ways. It separated us from God spiritually, caused our bodies to die physically, and cursed the earth (Genesis 3:6-19, 22-24). Yet despite humanity's disobedience, God is faithful and forgiving, and throughout history He has been enacting a plan to remove

Satan's dominion from the earth and redeem us. The scroll in this chapter is a particularly important part of that plan.

We know that Satan has temporary control over this world. He even offered that control to Jesus during the temptation in the wilderness, promising Him every earthly kingdom if Jesus would worship him (Luke 4:1-8). Jesus, being perfect God and understanding God's final plan for the earth, resisted temptation. If He had succumbed to temptation and sinned even once, He would no longer have been the spotless Lamb, able to redeem our spirits, our bodies, and the earth. He had the larger picture in mind, and resisted temptation so that we could all have the opportunity to be saved.

Scripture describes Satan as the small 'g' god of this world (2 Corinthians 4:3-4), but Jesus defeated him at the cross and we know that Jesus has the real authority over everything (John 12:31-33, Matthew 28:18-20). So, which is it? Does Satan still have dominion over the earth or is Jesus in control? The answer is yes (Hebrews 2:6-9). God has already given everything, all authority, to Jesus, but we have not seen the evidence of that complete control yet because Jesus is not exercising it. Everything is proceeding according to plan, and right now it is not yet time to redeem the earth (Acts 1:6-7). Therefore, God is allowing Satan some authority for just a little while longer.

Jesus will fully exercise the control that He already possesses when He redeems the earth. He has already begun this work by redeeming our spirits through salvation. The next step in our redemption is the redemption of our physical bodies, which will happen for the Church at the Rapture, and for the Old Testament and Tribulation saints at the end of the Tribulation. The redemption will be completed when the earth is redeemed, and the scroll represents the terms of that redemption. As Jesus opens each seal on the scroll, the world moves one step closer to redemption.

In the Old Testament, God gave us three laws that foreshadowed how He would redeem us in the end. The law of the redemption of the bride represents spiritual death being redeemed by salvation (Deuteronomy 25:5-10). That law said that if a man died and left his wife childless, a relative of his would take her as his wife and have children with her (as we see in the story of Ruth and Boaz). This process represents spiritual redemption. When we sinned, we were left alone and had no family to protect us. Jesus stepped in to save us and graft us into His family. When you receive salvation, you are spiritually made alive and you join the Bride of Christ (John 5:21-24, 2 Corinthians 11:2). Jesus redeems our spirits and makes us part of His family through salvation.

The second death that we must be redeemed from is the death of the physical body. Death is a result of sin, and our physical bodies will not be redeemed until we receive our new bodies. This process is represented by the law for the redemption of the slave (Leviticus 25:47-55). When we sinned, we enslaved our bodies and spirits to sin. Though our spirits have been redeemed through salvation, our bodies will remain slaves to sin until we receive our new bodies (Romans 6:3-4, 7:14-18). When we receive our new bodies, death will be fully defeated, and we will never die again (John 11:25-27). For people in the Church, that will happen at the Rapture, and for the rest of the saints, it will come at the end of the Tribulation.

The final consequence of the fall is the curse on the earth, and this is what Jesus will redeem as He opens the seals. God has the power to redeem the earth now, but He has planned since the beginning to redeem the earth after He completes the redemptions of body and spirit. This final redemption is represented in the Old Testament by the law of redemption of the land (Leviticus 25:23-28). If someone in the Old Testament lost their property, the only way they could get it back was if a close relative stepped up and bought it back for them. When that land was put up for sale, the terms of the redemption were written on a scroll and sealed (Jeremiah 32:6-15). This is so important: the scroll in Revelation five is the title deed of the earth! When Jesus takes the scroll, He is beginning the seven-year process of redeeming the earth from the curse of sin and Satan. After He redeems the earth, Jesus will set up His never-ending kingdom! Jesus must open the scroll because He is the only one worthy to fulfill the requirements for the redemption of the earth that are written on that scroll.

We had dominion over the land, but we lost it to Satan at the fall. The only way that we can get it back is if a close relative (our heavenly Father, and Jesus the Bridegroom) buys it back for us. Jesus must fulfill all the terms written on the scroll to redeem the earth. When Jesus takes the scroll in John's vision, all the elders and creatures begin to worship Him. They say that He is worthy to open the scroll, and that He will make us priests to reign on the earth that He buys back. At that time, Jesus will begin to redeem the earth. The earth yearns for the Rapture of the Church because it knows that after Jesus redeems our bodies, the earth's redemption will be next (Romans 8:18-25).

As we study each seal, you will see God fulfill every requirement that is necessary to redeem the earth. The redemption process will take place throughout the Tribulation time period. Satan will not relinquish the earth easily. He will fight to the end, but we know the outcome of the fight. At the end of the Tribulation, Jesus will exercise His full authority, and He will reign for ever and ever (Revelation 11:15-19).

Jesus is the only one who can open the scroll, and He is the only one who can redeem us. That might make you feel like you have no part in the redemption process, but this passage shows that we participate in this event through prayer (Revelation 5:8, 8:3). Our role in this process begins even now. Jesus has taught us from the very beginning to pray for that day to come. When Jesus taught His disciples to pray, He taught them to pray that His kingdom come on earth just as it exists in heaven (Matthew 6:9-10)! He wants us to pray for the redemption of the earth and the establishment of His eternal kingdom. All our prayers will add to His glory. We should ask daily for God's return and reign to bring lasting peace to Israel (Psalm 122:1-9). Start praying for that day to come. You won't be able to predict His return, but if you pray, you'll be ready for it. Come soon, Lord Jesus.

Chapter Three
The Sealing of the 144,000
Revelation 7, 14:1-5

Before Jesus begins to open the seals on the scroll, He will seal the 144,000. This raises a few questions: Who are the 144,000? What does it mean that they will be sealed? And how do we know that they will be sealed before Jesus opens the scroll? We know that these 144,000 will be sealed before Jesus begins to open the seals because their sealing occurs before the angels release the winds of destruction on the earth (Revelation 7:1-4). When Jesus begins to open the seals, He will redeem the earth by releasing these angels and sending judgments upon the earth. In Revelation chapter seven, the destruction described in Revelation chapter six hasn't been released yet. Therefore, the events described in Revelation chapter seven must occur before those of chapter six.

Our passage states that these angels have been given power to harm earth and sea (Revelation 7:2-3), but it doesn't specify why they are not yet allowing the winds to blow on the earth. Scripture has mentioned these winds elsewhere, and that is how we know that they will bring the destruction of the seals. Daniel spoke about these winds. In one of Daniel's visions, the four winds of heaven stirred up four beasts, which represented kingdoms that would bring judgment on Jerusalem (Daniel 7:1-8). Every time they appear in scripture, the winds represent God's judgment. The winds also appear in Jeremiah, during the destruction of Elam (Jeremiah 49:34-36). God promised to scatter Elam with the four winds of heaven, and in that way destroy them. The angels are holding the winds back in Revelation seven because they represent God's Tribulation judgment, and God has instructed the angels not to release it until the 144,000 servants of God are sealed and protected. This must happen before any seals on the scroll are opened.

Why are the 144,000 sealed *and protected* (Revelation 9:4)? People that receive salvation during the Tribulation judgment are not promised physical protection from God—in fact, many of them will be martyred for their faith (Revelation 6:9-11, 20:4). Believers will not be spared death at this time, but these 144,000 servants of God are different. God will seal them, and He will not allow harm to come to them. Why do they receive physical protection that other Tribulation saints don't? The answer lies in the identity and purpose of the 144,000.

The first thing the scripture says about the 144,000 is that they are servants of God (Revelation 7:3). It also says that the group of 144,000 consists of 12,000 people from each tribe of Israel (Revelation 7:4-8). We receive even more details about their identity in chapter fourteen of Revelation. They are virgins, and they follow Jesus the Lamb wherever He goes. We also learn that they are honest and blameless, and they are the firstfruits of those redeemed in the Tribulation (Revelation 14:4-5).

These isolated facts form a beautiful description when you put them together, so let's unpack each one! First, the 144,000 are Jews. The passage could not be any clearer—it even lists each of the twelve tribes of Israel. We are to take the Bible literally, so if the Bible says the 144,000 are Jews, don't let anyone tell you otherwise. We the Church are not the 144,000! The Church will not be present in the Tribulation to do what God has called the 144,000 to do. Additionally, most in the Church are not Jewish, and there are more than 144,000 believers in the Church! If you are in the Church, do not be disappointed that you are not a part of the 144,000; God has a great plan for the 144,000, but His plan for the Church is just as good. We in the Church Age can have a wonderful personal relationship with God that means that we will be Raptured before the Tribulation ever begins. If you were one of the 144,000, then you would not be involved in the Rapture, and you would have to endure the trials of the Tribulation! Thank God for His grace and your salvation in these days.

The 144,000 will be servants of God that follow the Lamb wherever He goes (Revelation 7:3, 14:4). This fact is intrinsically linked to two other facts about them: they are virgins, and they do not lie (Revelation 14:4-5). The reason scripture specifies that they are virgins is not because sex within marriage is wrong, because it isn't. It is very God-honoring in the correct context. Rather, they are celibate because God does not want them to be distracted by the responsibility of a wife and family; He wants these particular people to focus solely on the mission God has for them (1 Corinthians 7:32-34). Because they are virgins, they can follow God with no other obligations.

Their blamelessness and truthfulness are the final clues to the 144,000's purpose. They are Jewish servants of God, sealed and protected, and they go wherever God tells them to because they have no other attachments. As they go throughout the world, they speak the truth. It is paramount that they be truthful because God has set them apart to be witnesses throughout the world during the Tribulation. The 144,000 is a group of celibate male Jews that follow Jesus wherever He calls them to go; they will go throughout the world as missionaries, preaching the Gospel to anyone who will listen during the Tribulation. It is important that they are protected because the Gospel must go out.

Their testimony will play a part in the great multitude coming to faith during the Tribulation (Revelation 7:9-17). Zephaniah described the multitude as the 'daughters of the dispersed ones' (Zephaniah 3:10). The multitude will be from every tribe and nation and language, and they will be saved because of the 144,000 Jewish evangelists that will disperse throughout the world to share the Gospel. The role of the 144,000 is to witness to those in the Tribulation.

The 144,000 are called the 'firstfruits' from mankind because they will be the first people saved in the Tribulation (Revelation 14:4b). The term 'firstfruits' in the Bible is used to indicate that the subject is the first of its kind, but not the only of its kind. The 144,000 are the first representatives of what is to come. Jesus was described as the firstfruits of those who had risen from the dead (1 Corinthians 15:20), not because He was the first to ever rise from the dead (e.g., Lazarus, John 11:1-44; and Jairus' daughter, Mark 5:22-24, 35-43), but because He was the first to rise and *never die again*. He was the first of that kind, representative of those to come! Since He rose from the dead, we can live forever through the redeeming work of the Holy Spirit in us.

So then, since the saved 144,000 are the firstfruits of the Tribulation Period, it means that more of their kind are coming. More people will be saved during the Tribulation! This is further proof of their connection to the multitude described in Revelation 7:9-17. But more than that—if the 144,000 are the *first* believers during the Tribulation, then the Church must already be gone. The salt of the earth will be removed prior to the Tribulation (2 Thessalonians 2:6-7), before God seals the 144,000. We who believe during the Church Age will be raptured, taken out of the earth, before the Tribulation begins. The 144,000 will be the first converts during the Tribulation Period. They will be celibate male Jews whose role as servants of God will send them all over the globe as protected witnesses for Christ. Because of their ministry, a multitude of people from all tribes and languages and nations will come to faith in Jesus during the Tribulation Period.

God has planned to use the nation of Israel as His witnesses from the beginning (Isaiah 43:8-15). He wants to bless all other nations through them (Genesis 12:1-3, 18:18,

22:15-18). Israel was set apart to be His priests and witnesses to the world, but they went away from Him and worshipped others. Because of this, His favor left them for a little while (Isaiah 49:14-16). He brought judgment upon them and scattered them to Syria and Babylonia (2 Kings 17:6-23, 25:10-13), then gave them another chance. They missed that opportunity by not accepting Jesus as the Messiah, even though He fulfilled all prophecy about the Messiah's first coming.

Because the Israelites did not accept Jesus, God scattered them again, this time to all nations. But it was prophesied that in the end times, God would gather them back permanently (Jeremiah 31:8-9, 31-40). We are beginning to see this regathering in our day. In 1948, God made Israel a nation again. Slowly, Jews are returning to the land. The gathering is not yet complete, but when it is, God will fulfill His promise to use them as His witnesses. He made a promise to them, and He keeps His promises. He will not forsake them. They are His chosen people, and His declaration that they will be His witnesses will be fulfilled in the 144,000.

As God's children, grafted in for a time, the Church should have a heart for Israel. He has not fully gathered them yet, and they still have discipline ahead of them. But we the Church should not think that we are better than them. We should not read ourselves into prophecies of the last days that are clearly meant for Israel. We will not be in the Tribulation! We have been grafted into God's plan for a season to bring God glory and to make Israel jealous, but at the right time He will move the calling back to Israel, and God will fulfill the rest of His prophecies for Israel. These prophecies are literal, and they are coming. It is by God's provision that the tiny nation of Israel still exists at all (Malachi 3:6-7), and He has a plan for them. God will use them as His 144,000 witnesses in the Tribulation. Until that happens, pray for the peace of

Jerusalem, be looking for what comes next, and thank God for allowing you to be a part of His plan.

Chapter Four
The Seals of Judgment
Revelation 6

•••

The Four Horsemen
Revelation 6:1-8

After He seals the 144,000, Jesus will begin to open the scroll of the title deed of the earth. There are seven seals on this scroll. As Jesus opens each seal, a judgment will be released upon the earth. Each judgment is a step towards cleansing and redeeming the earth. Jesus will break the seals in a distinct order, but so close together that the effects of each seal will overlap. The first four seals will bring the Antichrist, war, famine, and death. The four living creatures (the cherubim) will be involved in orchestrating this period of judgment, under God's authority and direction.

Jesus will open the first seal, and one of the four living creatures will invite a rider on a white horse to come forth. Scripture depicts the rider on the white horse with a crown and a bow, but no arrows. He will not have weapons, but he will come to conquer. Some think that this rider is Jesus because his arrival will look similar to the description of Jesus' second coming (Revelation 19:11-16). Both figures have crowns and will arrive on white horses, but there's a crucial difference that proves that this rider is not Jesus.

The rider can't be Jesus because this person will have no weapons. He will have a bow but nothing to shoot with it. When Jesus came to earth the first time, He came in peace, but at His second coming, He will come to defeat His enemies. When Jesus comes back to the earth, He will defeat His

adversaries with a sword that comes out of His mouth
(Revelation 19:15). The person that will emerge during the first
seal will not have a weapon. This rider is not Jesus. The Bible
has told us who he really is. It is not surprising that this rider
will seem similar to Jesus on the surface; this figure is the
Antichrist, the one who will pretend to be the Messiah.

The Antichrist will come on the scene and win power
and authority, but he won't do it with warfare or force. He will
do it with cunning, flattery, deceit, and intrigue. That's why our
passage depicts him without weapons. When he first arrives on
the scene, he will appear to be a good world leader. There will
be a one-world government in the future. It will be made up of
ten kingdoms that will come together to form one government.
Another ruler will arise to join those ten world powers. This
ruler will depose three of the original ten kings and become
ruler of the world. In time, it will become clear that he is the
one we know as the Antichrist (Daniel 7:1-8, 15-28). He will
reveal his true nature when he reneges on all his good promises.

The Antichrist will make a covenant with many people,
including Israel, which is supposed to last for seven years. He
will keep the covenant for a little while, but he will break the
covenant at the midpoint of the Tribulation. He will desecrate
the temple by stopping sacrifices and claiming to be God
(Daniel 9:27). This abomination must occur before Jesus'
second coming (2 Thessalonians 2:1-10). Don't waste your time
trying to determine who the Antichrist will be. The Bible is
clear that he will not be revealed until after the rapture of the
Church. Trying to figure it out now is a fruitless task, because if
you are part of the Church, you will not be on earth when the
Antichrist is revealed.

When Jesus opens the first seal to begin the
Tribulation, the Antichrist will emerge to begin his campaign of
conquest. When Jesus opens the next seal, the second living
creature will call a red horse out. The rider of this horse will be

given permission to completely remove peace from the earth. Chaos will erupt during the Tribulation.

There is wickedness in the world right now, and it increases day by day. But as bad as the world is, it does not even compare to the horrors the Tribulation will bring. God is still holding sin back through the Holy Spirit in believers (Matthew 5:13). At the Rapture, the action of the Holy Spirit through His Church will be taken from the earth, and peace will be extremely hard to come by. By the time Jesus opens the second seal, peace will disappear completely. War will increase rapidly during this time, and people will murder each other without provocation. This chaos will grieve God, but He will still be in control.

God has used horsemen like this in His judgment before. In the Old Testament, Zechariah saw visions of the horsemen. He learned that God sent them out to assess the wicked nations (Zechariah 1:7-17). In Zechariah's next vision of the horses, we learn that these horses and their riders are the four winds of heaven, and they carry out God's wrath in the manner that He instructs them to (Zechariah 6:1-8). In Revelation, the white horse represents conquering, red connects to judgment, and black is famine. God uses these horses to enact the different facets of His judgment.

The horse that will come with the breaking of the third seal is black, and its rider will bring famine. In the Tribulation, it will take a full day's wages just to buy the ingredients for one loaf of bread (Revelation 6:6). The famine will multiply the chaos brought by the second horseman, and the chaos will stretch far beyond desperation for food. There will be no money for necessities like housing and gas, because all your money will go to buying food so you can survive. Because of this, there will be anarchy across the globe, and it will be the perfect setting for a one world government to form and the Antichrist to seize power. The removed peace will cause war, murder, and famine because people won't be focused on farming or distributing food. The effects of the seals will be interconnected.

When Jesus breaks the fourth seal, a pale, ashen horse will come out. This horse is the color of death, and it will bring death. Its rider will be given authority to kill a quarter of the earth's remaining population after the rapture. Calculating from population numbers of today, approximately one and a half billion people will die.[7] Death will be rampant in the Tribulation, but there will still be limitations to it (Matthew 24:21-22). God will not allow this fourth horseman to kill everyone. He will only be allowed to kill by the sword, famine, disease, and wild animals. The first two methods overlap with the second and third seals. Deaths that will seem to be caused by war, murder, and starvation will really be orchestrated by the horsemen, through the authority that God will allow them during that season.

God has stated that He will mete out judgment through famine, beasts, sword, and pestilence (Ezekiel 14:12-23). No matter how hard we pray for the world, this judgment is coming. However, that doesn't mean that we should stop praying! Not everyone will be saved from the Tribulation, but as you pray, God will lead you to witness to people, and He will use you to bring some of them to salvation. The judgment is imminent. It is coming to all who will be on the earth at that time, but God is faithful. He will deliver His people, the Church, from this Tribulation, and all who believe in Jesus Christ as Lord and Savior are part of His Church! God is bringing this judgment to purify Israel and prepare them for His return. All the remnant of Israel will be saved, but they

---

[7] Kessinger, Tony. *Things That Must Take Place: A Commentary on Revelation Chapters 4-22*. Tony Kessinger, 2013.

must first go through the horrors of the Tribulation with the rest of the world (Zechariah 13:8-9).

God promised Israel that He would never leave them nor forsake them (Deuteronomy 31:8, 1 Kings 6:13), and He is going to keep that promise. Even though Israel continues to stray from God, He is faithful to them, and He is not done with them. He will not wipe them out. Even after all the world's sin, God is still giving people a chance to receive salvation. God will spare those who believe in Him during the Tribulation Period, but that doesn't mean they won't experience the judgment or die. It means that their souls will be spared, even if their bodies aren't. God is a merciful and righteous judge, and even in the judgment of the Tribulation, He will give constant opportunities for people to join His kingdom.

This truth is important for us. Don't ignore it because you won't be present during the Tribulation—after all, the book of Revelation was written to the Church! We are supposed to know what Revelation says so that we can communicate this message to the lost. They will think we're crazy when we tell them what is to come. Some might claim the prophecies are only symbolic or have already been fulfilled. Be merciful to the mockers and naysayers. It's not our job to convince them, but God does call us to tell them. We need to know what the Bible says is coming next so that when things begin to happen around the globe, we can point to where the Bible said it would happen.

The Tribulation will be unlike anything the world has ever seen or will ever see again (Matthew 24:21), and the time before it begins is running short. Tell people what is to come, and then tell them that by Jesus' mercy, they can be saved before they must endure this. God is a just and merciful God, and He desires for all to receive salvation and escape torment.

God has promised to keep the Church from this coming time of trial (Revelation 3:10). Those who believe during the Church Age will not have to go through the Tribulation at all. Nevertheless, we are to know and share what will happen in that time, and patiently endure until the Rapture comes. Be unified with all those who genuinely believe that Jesus is God and Lord of their life. Spend time together in the Word and encourage each other as the day approaches (Hebrews 10:24-25). Do life together, grow together in your knowledge of Jesus, and love each other more.

●●●

Seal Judgments Five and Six
Revelation 6:9-17

The events of the first four seals will occur during the first half of the Tribulation Period. These events will be just "the beginning of the birth pains" (Matthew 24:6-8). They are the first contractions; the trials of the Tribulation will get more intense and painful before Jesus comes. Let's study the next two seals, their importance for us, and how they indicate that the birth pains will get worse.

When Jesus opens the fifth seal in Revelation chapter six, John sees under the altar the souls of those killed for their faith. They are seen asking for vengeance on those who still live on the earth. They are told to wait until all those who will be killed in the Tribulation are gathered, and then God will avenge them. These souls are not the Church; these people are those killed during the Tribulation, and the Church will not be a part of the Tribulation. These souls are those who will come to faith after the rapture and will be killed because of their faith. Jesus will save them spiritually, and there will come a day when He makes their robes white, and they will no longer cry (Revelation 7:13-17). Until that day comes, they will face persecution in the Tribulation.

The fact that these saints ask for vengeance is proof that they are not the Church. That is not the attitude that the current Church is called to have. Jesus and Stephen both demonstrated the attitude we are to have in this age. People mocked and assaulted Jesus while He was on the cross, yet He prayed for His accusers' forgiveness (Luke 23:32-37). They did not believe that He was the Christ or that they needed forgiveness, and they killed Him for His claims, yet He forgave them. Stephen followed Jesus' example. The Pharisees stoned him for his testimony, yet even as he was being killed, Stephen prayed for his murderers' forgiveness. The modern Church, like Stephen, is supposed to have Jesus' attitude from His first coming: "Father, forgive them, for they know not what they do" (Luke 23:34). The first time Jesus came, He did not come to condemn the world. He came to offer salvation, and the Church Age Church is called to desire others' salvation in the same way that Jesus did. Conversely, the Tribulation saints will be waiting for Jesus' second coming, when He will return to judge those who mistreated Israel, persecuted His Saints, and/or did not believe in His name. The cries of the souls under the altar align perfectly with the purpose that Jesus will have at His second coming.

We in the Church Age are not to wish condemnation on those who don't believe, like the Tribulation saints are doing in this passage. Stephen requested forgiveness for people even as they were killing him, and the person who oversaw the stoning, Saul, later became one of God's most faithful believers. What amazing forgiveness! Instead of praying for God to destroy evil people, we are called to pray intensely for Him to forgive and transform them. God's return may seem slow, but it isn't. He is waiting for more people to come to faith (2 Peter 3:9).

As a member of the Church, align your attitude with Jesus.' Pray for second chances, forgiveness, and faith. Have the same attitude towards criminals that you have towards your loved ones. God desires for <u>all</u> people to receive salvation. Understand that God will get His work done and let Him use you. We're still here because there are still people who need to know the good news, and God is waiting patiently for them. When the time is right, God will remove His Church and Spirit from the earth, and God's attitude towards unbelievers is going to change. People will still have opportunities to receive salvation, but those who reject salvation through Jesus Christ will be judged harshly. The souls crying out for the avenging of their blood come from the future time period of judgment, the Tribulation. Jesus will judge in that day (John 5:22-24), so they are not wrong to ask for vengeance. At the end of the Tribulation, Jesus will return to the earth, set up His throne of judgment, and at that time He will fulfill the request of the souls under the altar.

When Jesus opens the sixth seal, there will be a major shift in the events of the Tribulation. The breaking of this seal will cause such global and astronomical events that people will no longer be able to deny that it's an act of God. During the events of the first five seals, there is no record of anyone on earth acknowledging God. All those terrible things will happen, and most of the world will claim it's natural. They won't acknowledge that God is behind it until this sixth seal. When they see these things, however, they will have no choice but to recognize God's work. As a result, everyone on earth will hide from God because they want to escape His wrath.

Humanity will know that the Lamb of God is the one doing all these things because they will have been told by the 144,000, the two witnesses in Jerusalem (that we will learn about later), and the testimony of the Church. God gave us this message to share so that people might be saved in the Tribulation. Even if people do not accept the message when we tell them the first time, it will sink in when Jesus breaks the sixth seal. God will use you whether you get to see the results or not. Share the truth. The Spirit of God will decide when and where it takes root.

At the opening of the sixth seal, there will be an earthquake that will move every mountain and island. The sun will be darkened, the moon turned red, and stars will fall to the earth. Finally, the sky will roll up like a scroll. These cataclysmic events are what will cause the people of the earth to finally acknowledge that God is working. Everyone left on earth will hide in the mountains and wish to be killed by rocks falling on them, rather than face God's wrath.

In Matthew twenty-four, Jesus described an event that sounds remarkably like the events of the sixth seal, but it is not the same. Instead, it describes Jesus' return at the end of the Tribulation to gather the believers on earth at that time, those who will inhabit the Millennial Kingdom (Matthew 24:29-31). It is easy to get confused between this and the events of the sixth seal, because the physical natural disasters look similar. However, the events described here in Revelation six will occur during the middle of the Tribulation, and the events Jesus described in Matthew twenty-four will occur at the end of the Tribulation, right before the Millennial Kingdom is established. Why does God use such similar occurrences at two different events? Well, both instances mirror the events of the cross, when the sun went dark and an earthquake shook Jerusalem (Matthew 27:45-54, Luke 23:44-45). These events are signs that God is at work, and just as the earthquake at the cross let everyone know that Jesus was God, the earthquakes and other events in the Tribulation will show His power and signal His return.

God's power is mighty and terrifying. When He reveals Himself through these catastrophic events, people will have strong reactions to it. The people of the earth will try to hide from God like Adam and Eve did; they will even call out for rocks to fall on them and hide them from His sight. Unfortunately, this is not the right way to respond to the fear of the Lord, and because they will not turn to Jesus, they *will* be crushed by a rock: Jesus, the Chief Cornerstone (Matthew 21:42-44). There are four ways to approach the fear of the Lord, and only one is right. You can attempt to hide from God (Psalm 139:7-16), fight Him, or freeze in fear (Matthew 25:14-30), but none of those methods will succeed. The only proper response to a healthy fear of the Lord is to run *to* Him because He provides for your every need (Luke 12:4-7, 22-34). Run to Him for His protection. If you fall on the Cornerstone, you will be broken and rebuilt again, but if the Cornerstone falls on you, you will be crushed (Matthew 21:42-44).

Tell those who fear the Lord: run to Him. Fall on *Him*, don't make Him fall on you. The fear of the Lord is the beginning of wisdom (Proverbs 9:10), and perfect love casts out fear (1 John 4:18). When we run to Him and fall on Him in faith, He breaks us of what we were and makes us righteous (2 Corinthians 5:17). There is no need for those in the Church to fear God's punishment any longer. However, those in the Tribulation who do not turn to Him will have every reason to fear. With the seven seals of the Tribulation, God will get the world's attention, and unfortunately, many won't have the correct reaction to the fear of the Lord. When they reject God, the pain of judgment will increase. The worst is yet to come.

Chapter Five
The Midpoint of the Tribulation
Revelation 12:1-6

All the events that we have studied so far will occur during the first half of the Tribulation. The two witnesses will also begin their ministry during the first half of the Tribulation (Revelation 11:1-14), but we will cover them in greater detail in chapter eight of this book. In this chapter, we will begin to study the midpoint of the Tribulation. At the midpoint of the seven-year Tribulation, the woman Israel will flee from her attacker, the dragon. We know that Israel will flee at the midpoint of the Tribulation because she will be sheltered in the wilderness for 1,260 days after she flees the dragon. According to the Hebrew calendar that has 360 days in a year, 1,260 days equates to three and a half years. Now, you might wonder how we know that the Tribulation will last for seven years! To answer that question, and to gain some important insight on the midpoint of the Tribulation, let's study a prophecy in Daniel nine.

Gabriel told Daniel that seventy 'sevens,' or units of time, have been decreed for Israel to complete their transgression and atone for their sin (Daniel 9:24-27). The word 'seven' or 'week' in this prophecy acts like the English word 'dozen.' The word 'dozen' denotes that there are twelve of something, but it does not specify what there are twelve of. Likewise, 'seven' or 'week' in this passage denotes seven units of time, but it doesn't say whether that unit is days, weeks, months, or years. Fortunately, we can find the answer to that question by interpreting the part of this prophecy that has already been fulfilled. The first sixty-nine 'sevens' have already occurred. They began with a decree by Artaxerxes and ended 483 years later with the Triumphal Entry of Jesus into

Jerusalem. Therefore, each 'seven' is seven years long, because 483 years divided by sixty-nine equals seven years. Sixty-nine 'sevens' have been completed so far in history, but one is still yet to come. The Tribulation Period is the last decreed 'seven' that will complete Israel's atonement (Daniel 9:24).

We know that the first sixty-nine 'sevens' have been fulfilled because the Bible gave clear descriptions of what must happen at the beginning and the end of the first sixty-nine 'sevens.' There is only one set of events that perfectly meets the requirements that scripture laid out. Daniel prophesied that the seventy 'sevens' would begin when a decree was given to rebuild the city structures of Jerusalem, including the walls, streets, and plazas. He said that these building projects would be completed in times of distress (Daniel 9:25). Next Daniel said that the first sixty-nine 'sevens' (seven plus sixty-two 'sevens') would conclude when the Anointed One, the Messiah, came. After the first sixty-nine 'sevens' were over, that same Messiah would be put to death, cut off and left with nothing (Daniel 9:25-26). The last 'seven' is separate, both in the passage and in real life, from the first sixty-nine. The events described alongside the last 'seven' clearly have not happened yet. We will come back to study that 'seven' that is to come, but for a moment let's focus on the fulfillment of the first sixty-nine.

There are only two events in all of history that match up with the events listed as the beginning and end of the first sixty-nine 'sevens.' The first is the decree by King Artaxerxes, when he instructed Nehemiah to return to Israel and rebuild the city and wall of Jerusalem (Nehemiah 2:1-8). This decree fulfilled all the requirements mentioned in Daniel's prophecy— the decree gave Nehemiah permission to rebuild city structures, including the wall of Jerusalem, and the work was completed in times of distress. The surrounding nations did not want Jerusalem to be rebuilt. When Nehemiah was rebuilding the wall according to Artaxerxes' decree, he and all the other builders had to have their weapons ready as they built, as they held off attack from all sides (Nehemiah 4:9-23). There was an earlier decree by Cyrus to rebuild the temple in Jerusalem, but it does not fulfill the requirements laid out by Daniel, because Cyrus only allowed the Israelites to rebuild the temple, not the city. In fact, he forbade them from rebuilding Jerusalem (Ezra 1:1-4, 4:19-24).

The event that completes the first sixty-nine 'sevens' is the Triumphal Entry of Jesus into Jerusalem. This was the coming of the Messiah, and one week later, the Messiah was cut off when He was crucified on the cross (Daniel 9:26). Thank God Jesus' death was not permanent, but it did clearly complete the first part of the prophecy. You may wonder why the Triumphal Entry was the coming of the Messiah and not Jesus' birth. The Triumphal Entry was the true declaration of Jesus as Messiah and King. He had not been shy about His identity before this point, but this event fulfilled prophecy that declared Him to be King (Zechariah 9:9), and people went before Him declaring that He was the prophesied Son of David and the Messiah (Matthew 21:1-11). This was the official declaration of His coming, so it is the fulfillment of the prophecy.

Jesus' Triumphal Entry was the announcement of Jesus as the Messiah, the promised Savior of the Jews. This was the Jews' chance to accept Him as their King and keep the covenant they had made with God. Unfortunately, many of the Jews did not accept Him. Even though Israel knew what scripture said and studied many prophecies that pointed to Jesus, they did not acknowledge Him. As Jesus looked out over Jerusalem during the Triumphal Entry, He wept over it (Luke 19:41-44). He bemoaned that they hadn't understood the prophecies and scriptures. They did not accept Him as the Messiah, and so there was a pause in the progression of the seventy 'sevens.' Israel's covenant was put on hold to give the Gentiles an opportunity for salvation. We have been grafted into the new covenant that was prophesied to Israel (Jeremiah 31:31-33, Ezekiel 36:22-27, Romans 11:11-32). God has not forgotten or neglected His promises to Israel. God will complete all the things decreed for Israel right on schedule, but the clock is not ticking right now. The prophecy has not yet been completed, and God has planned one more 'seven' (the Tribulation Period) to fulfill His decree.

The amount of time between the initiation of the seventy 'sevens' prophecy and the end of the sixty-ninth 'seven' is 483 years, calculated by the ancient Hebrew calendar. If you are interested in the math, I encourage you to study it for yourself and read calculations done by other scholars! The math shows that God fulfilled this prophecy to the very day. Each 'seven' mentioned in Daniel nine is exactly seven 360-day years long, and so the last 'seven,' the Tribulation that has not happened yet, will also be seven years long (or 2,520 days). Therefore, the woman from Revelation twelve who will flee with 1,260 days left in the Tribulation will be fleeing at the exact midpoint of the seven-year Tribulation Period.

If God fulfilled the first sixty-nine 'sevens' to the day, it logically follows that He will fulfill the prophecy of the last 'seven' to the day as well. Like he did for the first sixty-nine, Daniel gave a description of what will happen at the beginning and the end of the last 'seven.' It will begin with the covenant made between many people (including Israel) and 'the prince who is to come' (i.e., the Antichrist), and it will end with the defeat of the Antichrist and Satan by God Himself (Daniel 9:27, Isaiah 10:20-23). Halfway through the Tribulation, though, the Antichrist will break the covenant that he will have made with Israel, putting a stop to sacrifice in the temple of Jerusalem and declaring himself to be God. This is the abomination of desolation, and this is what will cause the woman in Revelation twelve to flee for the wilderness (Matthew 24:15-22).

The woman in Revelation twelve is Israel. We have been working off that assumption throughout this chapter, but now let's study the proof. The woman is clothed with the sun, has the moon under her feet, and has a crown of twelve stars on her head. Remember: when we see symbolism in the Bible, we have been told somewhere else in scripture what the symbols represent. In one of Joseph's early dreams, he saw the sun, the moon, and eleven stars bowing down to him. His father Jacob (also called Israel) recognized the symbols in the dream for what they were: the family of Israel (Genesis 37:9-11). The sun was Jacob, the moon Rachel and Leah, and the eleven stars Joseph's brothers (with Joseph himself as the twelfth star). They are the first family of Israel; the sun, moon, and twelve stars represent Israel.

For further proof that the woman in this passage is Israel, we can look to the fact that she gave birth to Jesus. Jesus is the child in Revelation twelve; He is to rule all the nations, and He was caught up to God's throne, where He belongs and will rule from. He and God are one; it is His throne too, and He will rule with a rod of iron (Revelation 12:5). Clearly this verse is referring to Jesus because scripture describes Jesus as ruling with an iron rod at His second coming (Revelation 19:13-15, Psalm 2:6-9). The child is Jesus, and Israel is the woman. She will be threatened by the dragon, and this is what will cause her to escape to the wilderness for the second half of the Tribulation.

The dragon that will chase Jesus and Israel and will be unsuccessful in destroying them is Satan (Revelation 12:9). When our passage first mentions the dragon, it describes him with seven heads and ten horns (Revelation 12:3). This passage does not tell us what that means, but it has been explained elsewhere in scripture. The ten horns represent the ten kings of the one-world government that is yet to come (Daniel 7:7-8, 19-25). The seven heads are seven kingdoms that have ruled or will rule the world (Revelation 17:1-14). Five of the world kingdoms that these heads represent had already fallen by John's time (they are Egypt, Assyria, Babylon, Medo-Persia, and Greece), one was reigning at the time of John's visions (Rome), and one is still yet to come. There has not been a worldwide empire since Rome fell. The kingdoms and kings are depicted as part of Satan the dragon because his influence is behind all of them. The seventh world government will be made up of ten kings. The Antichrist will rise up and depose three of them, and the rest will give him control of the empire. He will reign in relative peace for three and a half years (Daniel 7:25), but when Satan indwells him at the midpoint of the Tribulation (Revelation 13:1-5), he will declare himself to be God, and the birth pains of the Tribulation will speed up.

After the first 1,260 days of the Antichrist's covenant with the many, at the midpoint of the Tribulation, Satan will be permanently kicked out of heaven and come to earth to indwell the Antichrist. This will cause the Antichrist to step into the temple and declare himself to be God. He will stop all sacrifice, and the remnant of Israel will flee to the wilderness to be sheltered for the remaining 1,260 days of the Tribulation. God's plan has been in place for all of eternity. Satan has tried and will keep trying to throw it off track, but he can't. Satan's choice to defy God will result in his eternal defeat. Do not follow Satan to destruction. Choose to worship God through faith in Jesus the Messiah and follow Him to eternal life.

If we watch the news with man's eyes, the world seems crazy and out of control. It is easy to fall into panic and forget that God is sovereign. Instead, look at each event through the eyes of God. Everything that happens in the news, though it may seem horrible, is a step towards the completion of God's plan. Everything is right on schedule, and God is in control.

Chapter Six
Satan Cast to Earth
Revelation 12:7-17

Just before the midpoint of the Tribulation there will be a battle in the angelic realm between Michael and his angels and Satan and his fallen angels. Satan will be defeated in this battle, and this defeat is what will cause him to be cast to earth and instill his influence in the Antichrist. After that battle, Satan will no longer be allowed to even set foot in heaven (right now, he still appears before God to give reports—Job 1:6-7). Satan will realize then that his time is short. As a result, he will try to destroy as many people as he possibly can in the time that he has left. He will chase Israel into the wilderness using the Antichrist, and only one third of God's people will survive the attack and pursuit (Zechariah 13:8). He won't be able to reach the remnant of Israel once they are protected in the wilderness, so he will instead go after any person who believes in Jesus. The persecution of the Tribulation saints will increase exponentially during the last three and a half years of the Tribulation.

This chapter of Revelation describes Satan as a serpent as well as a dragon with seven heads and ten horns. These descriptions are consistent with other depictions of him throughout the Bible. In fact, it is likely that Satan took the form of some type of dragon in the Garden. We always think of him as a serpent like a snake, but it's possible that snakes in their current form didn't exist until after the fall. When God cursed Satan after he tempted Adam and Eve, He said that Satan *would* crawl on his belly and eat the dust of the earth (Genesis 3:14-15). It seems that before the fall of man, the creatures that became snakes did not slither on the ground. They were a type of serpent that had legs—perhaps, a dragon.

Other depictions of dragons in the Bible consistently point to Satan. A dragon like the one described in Revelation twelve really existed at one time (Job 41:1-11). God created an animal that represented Satan so that He could demonstrate His mastery over Satan. This animal was called the Leviathan. The Leviathan was not an alligator or crocodile, as you can tell if you examine its scriptural description. It was a fire-breathing dragon. God made an animal that humans could not defeat. He did this to challenge man's assumption that he could rival God. If humanity couldn't even master that animal, how could we presume to master God?

People on earth stayed far away from the Leviathan. They had no defense against its strength and fire. Have you ever wondered why so many ancient cultures share stories and lore about fire-breathing dragons? It's not a coincidence; at least one really existed, and it inspired the tales. The Leviathan doesn't exist anymore because God killed it (Psalm 104:24-29). He crushed Leviathan's heads (Psalm 74:12-14). Do you see what the scripture said? Leviathan had multiple heads. It is possible that Leviathan had seven heads like the dragon in Revelation twelve, but the scriptures do not say for sure. Leviathan may not have looked exactly like the fire-breathing dragons we imagine, with wings and a single head, but the Bible says that he was a fire-breathing dragon, so believe what the Word says.

Job described the Leviathan as a terrifying beast, strong in frame, neck, and limb (Job 41:12, 22, 25-29). No weapon of man could master it (Job 41:1-8). It had a leathery, scaly hide that could not be pierced or separated (Job 41:15-17, 23). Even its underbelly, an area that is soft on most animals, was spiny and dangerous (v. 30). Its eyes were reptilian, slitted, and glowing (v. 18) and its heart was hard as a stone (v. 24). It had a strong mouth with terrifying teeth (v. 14), and it breathed fire out of its mouth (v. 18-21). It made the sea boil (v. 31), and it

48

swam incredibly fast (v. 32). This sea-dwelling, fire-breathing dragon was a terror to behold. Praise God that He has killed Leviathan! Yet the Bible speaks in the future tense when it says that during Israel's redemption, God *will* punish Leviathan and slay the dragon (Isaiah 27:1). In this context, Leviathan is used as a metaphor for Satan in a passage about God's final defeat of Satan. This verse describes an event that is yet to come.

Revelation twelve describes Satan as a dragon with seven heads and ten horns. There is another beast described in Daniel seven and Revelation thirteen that has ten horns and seven heads (Daniel 7:7-8, 19-24, Revelation 13:1-8). This beast is not Satan, but it has the same number of heads and horns because Satan empowers it. The beast described in Daniel seven and Revelation thirteen is the coming one-world government that the Antichrist will lead, and the Antichrist will be indwelt by Satan, the dragon himself. The beast and the dragon are so intertwined that they are difficult to separate, and that is why they are described similarly. Satan is the driving force behind this coming government, and he will indwell the authority figure, the Antichrist, at the midpoint of the Tribulation (Revelation 13:2-4). Satan will cause him to be able to perform miracles and acts that will deceive people into thinking he is God (Revelation 13:3). Everyone who does not believe in the true God will be deceived, and the consequences will be horrific (Revelation 13:8).

Satan has been waging war on God since the beginning of time on the earth (1 John 3:8). Michael and the angels' defeat of Satan will be major, but Satan will fight God and lose a couple more times before he is put away forever. God is in control of every fight, and always has been. He knew that Satan would rebel, and He knows that Satan will not win the war that he initiated by his rebellion. God has known the choices Satan would make since before the foundation of the world, and He is equipped to handle it.

Throughout this war, both God and Satan have used humans in the fight. God created Satan to be a cherub, but Satan was not satisfied with the role God chose for him (Ezekiel 28:11-15, Isaiah 14:12-14). Satan thought that he was equal to God and tried to take over. Because of this arrogance, Satan lost his glorious position in heaven. Satan's temptation and the first sin filled humanity with the same attitude of pride, but God has given us a choice. We can decide we don't need Him like Satan did, or we can turn to God and follow Him. Both Satan and God want us to choose to worship them, but God is the only one who loves us and will be the right choice in the long run. Satan hates us and wants to destroy us. We are made in God's image, and Satan is so venomous against God that he can't stand anything that even looks like Him.

Our lives are being watched by more than just the world. We are an important part of the battle in the heavenly places. God created humans for His glory and in His image. He uses the Church to display His glory to the angels, both the good and bad ones (Ephesians 3:8-10, 1 Peter 1:10-12). Angels are interested in us because God does some things in us specifically to pique their interest. Remember: you are in a battle right now against Satan and his demons. God wants to work in you to display His power to them. You can't win on your own (Ephesians 6:10-12). That's why you must daily renew your mind and submit yourself to God (Romans 12:1-2). Resist the devil, and he will flee; not from you, but from Jesus who lives in you and works through you (James 4:7, 1 John 4:4).

The battle is bigger than you and has been going on for longer than you can fathom. God has a plan, and the war will play out exactly as He intends. The question is: are you going to complain because you're not satisfied with your role like Satan, or will you be like Jesus and accept God's plan, even if it means submitting to something that doesn't align with your plan?

Satan was given a beautiful, honorable role as a cherub, but he thought he deserved more. Don't be like him. Be like Jesus and submit yourself to the Father, even unto death.

We have learned about battles that have happened, a war that is waging all the time, and a battle that is still future, but there will be more battles after Satan is permanently cast to earth. There will be some earthly skirmishes, but at the end, God will smite Satan and his angels with fire and end the war. Then God will cast them into the Lake of Fire for eternity (Revelation 20:1-3, 7-10). We studied this long war for one reason: We know who wins. The Bible has told us that God will be victorious, and faith is not a gamble when you know who's going to win. Put all your hope and faith in Him. God is going to win.

Chapter Seven
The Antichrist and Satan
Revelation 13:1-10

This passage reveals a little more about the Antichrist, the one world government that he will rule, and those who will worship the Antichrist. The government and the Antichrist are depicted in this passage as a great beast that emerges from the sea. Satan will empower this beast, and this government will be Satan's last attempt to conquer all believers and rule over the entire world (Revelation 12:13-13:1). He will succeed in deceiving all who do not believe in Jesus until Jesus returns to set up His eternal kingdom.

Satan, the one world government, and the Antichrist are so interconnected that they are all described as creatures with ten horns and seven heads. Satan is described as a dragon and both the Antichrist and the one world government as a terrifying beast, but the ten horns and seven heads mean the same thing in every iteration. The seven heads refer to the seven kingdoms that have ruled or will rule the world, and the ten horns are ten kings that will arise to lead the last world kingdom (Revelation 17:8-14). At the end of time, there will be one more one world government. It will be made up of ten kingdoms that will come together to rule as one. The Antichrist is depicted as a horn that rises amongst those ten kings and plucks three out (Daniel 7:7-8, 19-25). When the Antichrist appears, he will depose three of the original ten kings, and the rest will give their allegiance and authority to him. He will then rule over the kingdom with Satan's authority for three and a half years (Daniel 7:25).

The final one world government is described as a beast in the books of Revelation and Daniel. Daniel was given a vision of four beasts, each representing a different world government (Daniel 7:1-8). The first beast Daniel saw was like a lion; it had wings, but they were taken from it. The beast was raised to stand on two feet and given the mind of a man. This beast is Babylon. Babylon was represented in ancient days by winged lions. The next beast in Daniel's vision looked like a bear. One side of this beast was larger than the other, and it ate ribs and flesh. This beast is Medo-Persia, and this empire came in to defeat and conquer Babylon. The larger side of the bear represents Persia and the smaller the Medes, and together they devoured many nations. The third beast was like a leopard with four heads and four wings. This is Greece. Alexander the Great expanded Greece to a great empire, but after his death, his four generals divided the land into equal kingdoms, represented by the four heads of the leopard.

Finally, Daniel saw a fourth beast that he did not have an animalistic description for, because it was so terrifying. The only way he could think to describe it was to say that it trampled and devoured everything in front of it. Other than its behavior, one of the only descriptors we are given is that it has ten horns. Then another horn rises up and uproots three of the ten—again, depicting the Antichrist. In Revelation thirteen, the beast that comes out of the sea has ten horns, just like the beast in Daniel seven. The beast described in Revelation also has seven heads. Revelation thirteen describes the beast as a leopard with the feet of a bear and the teeth of a lion. As you can see, this new beast will have characteristics of all three kingdoms that came before it, but it will be different and more terrifying.

Satan will give this beast his power, throne, and authority. The last one world government will be orchestrated by Satan, and its leader the Antichrist will be empowered by Satan. First the Antichrist will go after the Israelites, and he will succeed in killing a lot of them, but the remnant will be protected in a place that he cannot reach. Once the Antichrist can no longer reach the Israelites, he will go after everyone on earth who is a believer in God and Jesus Christ, as Satan directs him to do (Revelation 12:17).

The Bible says that in that time, whoever is to be captured or killed **will** be captured or killed. There will be no physical deliverance during this time, but God calls believers in the Tribulation to endure in their faith despite the horrible circumstances (Revelation 13:9-10). The beast will be allowed at that time to physically conquer the saints (Revelation 13:7, Daniel 7:21). It will be worse than anything we can imagine, but it will have limitations. If God had not promised to limit this intense persecution to three and a half years, not a single person would remain alive on the earth after the Antichrist's reign (Matthew 24:15-22). We cannot even fathom the scope of this persecution and suffering.

Those who don't believe in Jesus, and thus will not be targeted by the Antichrist, will end up worshipping Satan, who empowers the beast. They will think he is invincible (Revelation 13:4). They will be wrong about that. Jesus has conquered Satan. He was predestined to crush Satan's head (Genesis 3:15). He defeated Satan at the cross, and at the end of the Tribulation, Jesus will bind Satan in the pit for a thousand years (Revelation 20:1-3). Satan will only come out of the pit because God will allow it, and then He will immediately defeat Satan once and for all (Revelation 20:7-10). Jesus is greater than Satan, who will empower the beast to do its damage.

God has also empowered Michael and His angels to defeat Satan (Revelation 12:7-8). They will do their part by casting Satan down to earth until it is time for Jesus to bind him in the pit. In the meantime, there is another group who can defeat him, and that is the Tribulation believers. Even though Satan may seem to win because he will kill a lot of them, the Tribulation saints are the true conquerors because they will stand strong in their salvation and testimony, and they will not be defeated even in death (Revelation 12:10-11). Satan knows that their physical deaths will be a hollow victory for him, because after believers die, they pass on to glorious eternal life.

The Tribulation saints will be able to conquer Satan by the blood of the Lamb and the word of their testimony because they will not value their lives more highly than they value their faith. Church Age believers should learn from them. When Satan tempts or worries us, he often does it by threatening our life and the comforts of this world. If we value our lives like the Tribulation saints will (i.e., not at all), this hold that he has over us disappears. When this world loses its appeal, Satan has nothing to attack you with (Philippians 4:11-13). Submit yourself to God and His ways, and the devil will flee because he knows he is conquered (James 4:7). When Satan wins in our lives, it's because we get focused on this life. Focus instead on the life to come.

When the false worshipers say, "Who is able to stand against the beast?" The answer is: Jesus, who has already done it and will do it again, the angels, who will do it at the midpoint of the Tribulation, and every believer who trusts in the Lord and does not put their treasure in this life. Unfortunately, the beast's worshipers will not recognize this truth, and they will not worship Jesus as Lord and Savior of their lives. That's why their names were never written in the Lamb's Book of Life (Revelation 13:8).

The names of those who honestly believe in Jesus have been written in the Book of Life of the Lamb since before the world was created. There are many references to this book throughout the Bible. Paul also said believers' names were written in the Book of Life (Philippians 4:3). At the Great White Throne Judgment, those who do not believe will be judged by their works and thrown into the Lake of Fire, because their names won't be found in the Book of Life (Revelation 20:11-15).

Revelation confirms in multiple places that the people who worship the beast do not have their names written in the Book of Life, which was written before the foundation of the world (Revelation 17:8). There are some other verses that call this book the "Book of Life of the Lamb." In one of those verses, we learn that only those whose names are written in the Lamb's Book of Life will be able to live in the New Jerusalem (Revelation 21:27). And as our passage says, only those who are not written in the Lamb's Book of Life will worship the beast (Revelation 13:8). All the descriptions of the Book of Life and the Book of Life of the Lamb align: those who believe in Jesus are written in the book and will receive eternal life, and those who don't believe in Jesus are not written in the book and will face eternal punishment. The two titles refer to the same book.

The Bible says in a couple of places that the names of the righteous were written in this book before the foundation of the world. God knew who would be in it from the beginning. So, can you ever have your name blotted out of the book? Surprisingly, the answer is yes. Our passage says that the false worshipers' names were never in the book, but the whole of scripture reveals that the answer is a little bit more complicated than that.

Jesus promises that He will not blot those who walk with Him out of the Book of Life, thereby implying that He could blot them out if He decided to (Revelation 3:4-5). But there is more proof that God can edit the Book. God told Moses that He would blot anyone who sinned against Him out of His Book (Exodus 32:30-33). There is a similar indictment of the unrighteous elsewhere (Psalm 69:25-28). So how can someone's name be blotted out of the Book, but at the same time have never been written in it, as our passage says? The answer goes back to the debate Christians have been having for eons: God's foreknowledge versus human free will. It is important to not go too far to one side or the other of that debate. Our mistake has been thinking that the two are mutually exclusive. In the human mind they are, but God can make room for both in His plan. Man has a choice, but God determines who will be saved (Acts 13:42-48).

From looking at all the passages about the Book of Life, it is clear: everyone has a choice. I believe you are put in the Book of Life from the moment you are conceived. There comes a day when you are faced with a choice of believing in Jesus or not, and if you miss your opportunity, you are wiped out of the Book. And because God knows everything before it happens, it can simultaneously be that those who reject Jesus were never in the Book. God has not predetermined which individuals will receive salvation and which won't; he offers the choice to all (John 3:16-18). At the same time, He does know how everyone will respond, and He has recorded it in His Book of Life. This balance does not erase either our responsibility or His omnipotence. God's forgiveness stretches to all. The only sin Jesus' death did not cover is the blasphemy of the Holy Spirit, otherwise known as when the Spirit draws you and you reject Him (Matthew 12:31-32). That is the only thing that can keep you from being written in the Book of Life.

Stay away from the extremes; as we have just seen, the Bible says that you can be blotted out of the Book if you reject Christ, and it also says that you cannot lose your salvation once you have it (John 10:28-30, Ephesians 1:13-14). You are eternally secure if you are in Christ (Revelation 3:4-6). Everyone has an opportunity to believe, but God knows who will and He recorded it before the foundation of the world. God can handle the apparent dichotomy. If you choose not to receive Jesus' forgiveness and you sin against Him, God will blot you out of His Book. If you get blotted out, you were never really in the Book, because He knew you wouldn't be. It could make your head explode if you think about it too hard, so rest in the fact that you don't have to fully understand it. God does, and that's enough. Let me put it to you this way: God already knows the choice you'll make about following Jesus, but you don't! Make the right choice.

Chapter Eight
Prophets, Both Real and False
Revelation 11:1-14, 13:11-18, 14:6-13

•••

The Two Witnesses
Revelation 11:1-14

There will be so much deception and even a false prophet from Satan during the Tribulation, but God will provide people to speak the truth as well. In addition to the 144,000 Jewish witnesses that we have already talked about, God will provide two prophets that will proclaim the truth during the Tribulation Period. These prophets will begin prophesying from Jerusalem early in the Tribulation Period, and their ministry will continue for three and a half years. At the midpoint of the Tribulation, they will be killed by the Antichrist, resurrected by God, and then called up to heaven (Revelation 11:7-12).

The prophets will prophesy from Jerusalem because God will send these prophets specifically to the nation of Israel, to plead with them to repent. At the beginning of Revelation chapter eleven, John was instructed to measure the temple in Israel. At the time of John's vision, there was no physical temple in Israel. The Romans had destroyed the temple approximately twenty years before. The temple John saw and measured in our passage is the one that will exist in Jerusalem during the Tribulation. He was told not to measure the outer courts where the Gentiles are permitted to worship, but to measure the temple, the altar, and those who worship there (Israel). This symbolizes God measuring the spiritual state of the Israelites, and because they will not measure up to God's standards, God will send His two witnesses to prophesy to them for three and a half years. God wants His people to come to know Him. The two witnesses will plead with Israel to repent.

The witnesses will be clothed in sackcloth, which denotes repentance in the Bible (Matthew 11:20-21). Dressing in sackcloth and ashes showed that you were humbling yourself, and that your repentance was sincere. When the people of Nineveh repented of their sin, they even draped sackcloth on their animals. The witnesses being dressed in sackcloth indicates that their message to Israel will be one of humility, repentance, and brokenness. They will call on the Israelites to return to God sincerely, not just in name or appearance. There may be a new temple in Israel at that time, but that does not mean that Israel will truly be righteous before God.

God has planned for these prophets to come for a long time. Our passage describes them as olive trees and lampstands that stand before the Lord of the earth. This exactly echoes a prophecy given by Zechariah that decreed that the olive trees and lampstands were anointed ones who stand by the Lord (Zechariah 4:1-3, 11-14). These two prophets have been set aside for this very purpose. They will come to witness to Israel and plead with them to repent and return to God, but they will face opposition. They will preach nonstop, and that will create enemies. Yet, God will protect them throughout the course of their ministry. When people try to stop the prophets from teaching before their time is complete, fire will come out of the prophets' mouths and consume their attackers. Yet after three and a half years of ministry, the beast will strike them down and kill them. God will protect them for exactly as long as He has planned for them to testify, and then He will allow them to die so that He can complete His plan for them.

They will lie unburied in the streets for three and a half days as the world celebrates their death by giving gifts to one another. After those three and a half days, they will come back to life, and it will terrify those who see it happen. Then a voice from heaven will call them away, and they will be raptured before the world's eyes! God will call them to heaven with the same words that John heard in Revelation 4:1— "Come up here!"

The scripture is clear about the prophets' purpose and what will occur at the end of their ministry, but this passage raises two more questions. When exactly will their ministry occur, and who are the two prophets? A couple of hints from our passage will help us discern the timeline of their ministry. The prophets' ministry must begin before the midpoint of the Tribulation because their ministry will last for exactly three and a half years (Revelation 11:3). If their ministry begins at the midpoint of the Tribulation, there will not be time left at the end for them to lay dead for three and a half days and then be resurrected. Additionally, our passage says that the events that will occur after their death and resurrection are only the end of the second woe; there is a third woe (i.e., more events of judgment) still to come (Revelation 11:12-14). There must be enough time left in the Tribulation after their ministry is over for the third woe to occur.

It also makes sense that the majority of the two witnesses' ministry in Jerusalem will occur during the first half of the Tribulation, because their message is to the Jews, and the Jews will flee Jerusalem at the midpoint of the Tribulation Period. I tend to believe that their ministry will begin at the start of the Tribulation and that the Antichrist will strike them down as he steps into the temple to desolate it, and then God will resurrect them three and a half days into the second half of the Tribulation Period. However, the Bible does not say exactly when their ministry begins and ends, so I do not claim a specific timeline.

If the witnesses are who I believe they are, they will come from the presence of God to the earth for this purpose. People love to speculate about who the two witnesses might be, but the Biblical answer is: we don't know for sure. Keeping this important distinction in mind, I would like to show you the Biblical evidence for who I believe the two witnesses are.

I believe the two witnesses will be Elijah and Moses. In our passage, we see that the witnesses can miraculously stop the rain. God can give that power to anyone He chooses, but we know that He gave that power to Elijah when he was prophesying to Ahab (1 Kings 17:1). Not only that, but Elijah stopped the rain for three and a half years when he prayed to God, exactly the length of the witnesses' testimony (James 5:17, 1 Kings 18:1). That's some foreshadowing for you! The witnesses are also able to turn water into blood and inflict plagues, just like Moses during the Egyptian Captivity (Exodus 7-12). These are good hints about who the witnesses will be, but there is even more convincing evidence.

Moses and Elijah appeared in glory with Jesus at the Transfiguration (Matthew 17:1-8). The Bible says that the Law and the Prophets testify to the identity of Jesus Christ (Romans 3:21-22). Moses wrote the entirety of what the Hebrews call the Pentateuch (the Law), while Elijah is one of the most prolific Old Testament prophets. When Moses and Elijah stood by at the Transfiguration while God declared that Jesus was His son, the Law and the Prophets were literally testifying that Jesus is God. I believe that they will again testify on Jesus' behalf as the two witnesses in the Tribulation.

There is also a prophecy that says God will send Elijah before the day of the Lord, and Elijah will turn the hearts of fathers toward their children (Malachi 4:5-6). John the Baptist came before Jesus' first coming as a type of Elijah, having the spirit and power of Elijah, and he turned the hearts of fathers to their children, just as the prophecy said (Luke 1:13-17). John was a type of Elijah, but he only fulfilled the prophecy partially. Even after John the Baptist's completed ministry, Jesus said that Elijah was still to come, and that he would restore all things (Matthew 17:9-13). Elijah did come in the form of John the Baptist, and Israel did whatever they wanted to him. Still, Elijah himself will come again, and he will restore all things. I believe that Elijah will come again as one of the two witnesses, and in that way, complete the prophecy.

I believe the Bible gives strong clues to the identities of the two witnesses, but who the witnesses are doesn't matter as much as what their role is. God will speak through the two witnesses about man's need for repentance and reconciliation with God. They will be sent to the nation of Israel to point them back to God. They will preach in Jerusalem, clothed in sackcloth, for three and a half years. The world will hate them so much that they will rejoice when the Antichrist kills them. Despite that apparent defeat, God will prove He is still in control by raising them from the dead after three and a half days.

We in the Church have been given a role much like that of the two witnesses (2 Corinthians 5:18-21). We are ambassadors for Christ, and our job is to tell people that Jesus died so that they could be forgiven. We are to plead with them to reconcile with God. In God's ledger, the price has been paid for everyone's sin, but that doesn't mean that everyone goes to heaven (Colossians 1:19-20). Through Jesus, God has paid the cost of your forgiveness; now you must acknowledge Him as Lord and accept His gift of salvation. If you do, you will spend eternity with God and have your name written in the Book of Life. God does not wish for anyone to perish. God loves you, and He's paid for your sin. Receive that gift by accepting Him as your Savior and being sealed by the Holy Spirit, and then plead with others to be reconciled with God the way you have been. Be an ambassador for God like these two witnesses.

•••

The False Prophet
Revelation 13:11-18, 14:6-13

The beginning of Revelation chapter thirteen introduced a beast that will emerge from the sea, and we learned that that beast is the Antichrist. We know that this beast will take control of the world and will be empowered by Satan himself (Revelation 13:1-5). Now, the second half of Revelation chapter thirteen introduces a second beast. This beast will rise out of the earth instead of the sea. It has two horns like a lamb, but don't be fooled. It is not a lamb. It speaks like the dragon, Satan. This beast will come in a deceptively nonthreatening, peaceful, and religious form, but its message will be born of Satan.

It becomes clear that this beast is not from God when you compare it to the two prophets that we just learned about. The two witnesses' message of repentance will match their actions, down to the sackcloth that they wear. The second beast's words will be at odds with his actions. Jesus warned us about people like this, who look one way and act another (Matthew 7:15-20). He called them false prophets, because they appear to be religious and claim to speak for God, but they spread lies. Jesus told us to examine spiritual teachers' lifestyles because that will reveal whether they are of the truth. If they are prone to fits of rage, dissension, envy, or strife, they are of the flesh and not the Spirit (Galatians 5:19-21). If their life does not match their speech, they are not from God.

This beast that rises out of the earth is called the False Prophet. We get this name from three places in Revelation

(Revelation 16:13, 19:20, 20:10). In all three places, the False Prophet is mentioned in conjunction with the Antichrist and Satan. The dragon, the Antichrist, and the False Prophet form a false or unholy trinity that copies and perverts the true Holy Trinity of God the Father, Jesus the Son, and the Holy Spirit. Satan will build his own unholy trinity because he cannot create anything new. Satan wants to be God so badly that he emulates what God does, but his version of God's plan is twisted and cannot measure up to God's divine plan.

There is only one God, but He manifests Himself in three persons: The Father, the Son, and the Holy Spirit. The Father is the authority. Jesus is the Son, and even though He is fully God, He submitted Himself to the Father while He was on the earth. He did whatever the Father would have Him do (John 5:19, 30). Jesus did nothing by His own power, although He could have. Instead, God the Father empowered Jesus while He was on the earth (John 14:10). God the Father empowers the Son, and the Holy Spirit's role is to bring glory to the Son, thereby glorifying the Father as well. All three aspects of God work together to form the complete picture. Conversely, in the Tribulation, Satan will empower the Antichrist, and the False Prophet will bring glory to the Antichrist. The False Prophet will make the inhabitants of the earth worship the Antichrist, and therefore they will worship Satan who empowers him. Satan is not creative, but he is devious and deceitful. He wants to pull people away from God's design and trick them into following his perversion of God's design.

One of the reasons that the False Prophet will be able to convince the world to worship the Antichrist is because the Antichrist will appear to recover miraculously from a mortal wound. We don't know exactly what the Antichrist's 'mortal wound' will be, but we know why it is important. A mortal wound is a wound that is so serious it leads to death. You should not be able to recover from a mortal wound. Nevertheless, the Antichrist's mortal wound will be healed, and the world will be in awe (Revelation 13:3). This wound will be so severe that the Antichrist will die, or at least appear to die. Therefore, it will shock the world when he is healed. Again, Satan cannot create anything new. This false resurrection is an attempt to copy Jesus' death and resurrection, but as always, Satan's copy will fall short.

When this false miracle is performed, the False Prophet will convince the inhabitants of the earth to worship the Antichrist because of his resurrection and the other miracles that God will allow the False Prophet to perform, like calling down fire from heaven. Those miracles do not mean he is from God; remember, Pharaoh's magicians copied Moses and Aaron's sign from God (Exodus 7:8-13). The Antichrist and False Prophet are going to be able to do things that are miraculous and awe-inspiring. They will fool a lot of people (Matthew 24:23-27). The False Prophet will also tell people to erect an image of the Antichrist, and God will allow the False Prophet to give this idol breath so that it will speak. These events will convince most of the world that the Antichrist is a god, and they will worship him. Those who do not worship the beast will be killed.

The False Prophet will force people to take the mark of the beast. The mark will be the name of the Antichrist, or the number of the Antichrist's name, which is 666. Don't try to guess the Antichrist's name based on this number or try to predict who he might be. The Bible says he won't be revealed until after the Rapture, and hopefully you will not be on earth when he is revealed (2 Thessalonians 2:1-8). We do not know exactly what form the mark will take; it "calls for wisdom" (Revelation 13:18). God has not yet revealed this mystery. People for years have tried to figure out what the mark will be. If it were possible to know exactly what the mark will be, I

believe we would know. Don't waste time guessing. It will
become clear when the time is right.

At that time, if anyone refuses to take the mark, they
will be cut off from the normal functions of life such as buying
and selling, and they will be killed (Revelation 13:16-18, 20:4).
Everyone on earth will have to decide. There will be no
avoiding this situation. Additionally, no one will be ignorant of
what the choice means. The Antichrist will not trick people into
taking the mark. At that point in the Tribulation, the entire
world will have clearly heard the Gospel. Not only will they
have the testimony of the 144,000 and the two witnesses, but
God will also send an angel to preach the Gospel to the whole
world (Revelation 14:6-7, Matthew 24:14). The angel will
entreat people to fear God and worship Him. Those who
choose not to worship the beast and do not take the mark will
be signing their own death warrant, but the Bible says that they
will live on spiritually, which is the only life that truly matters. If
you are willing to be put to death for the sake of the true
Christ, Jesus will bring you back to life when He sets up His
kingdom physically on the earth.

Anyone who chooses to take the mark, though they
may live physically for a little while longer, will be eternally
condemned (Revelation 14:9-11). If you take the mark, that
means that you are actively choosing to glorify and worship
Satan via the Antichrist, and you will be signing your eternal,
spiritual death warrant. I pray that none of you will be on the
earth during that time, but if you are, consider the eternal
consequences of the choice, not just the immediate
consequences. If you know you won't be on the earth to face
this decision, warn others about it. They may not believe now,
but they'll remember what you said and come to know the
truth later. Know what the Bible says now and believe in Jesus
today so that you can escape those days. If you choose to reject
God's offer of salvation, please know that believing in the truth

during the Tribulation Period will be exceedingly difficult. God will send a strong delusion to those in the Tribulation so that they will be fooled by the Antichrist and his False Prophet (2 Thessalonians 2:8-12). That is why God gives a blessing to those who will refuse the mark and face martyrdom (Revelation 14:12-13). They will have to endure many more trials, but they will receive reward for their faith in Jesus. Believe today, so that you won't have to face those trials!

At the False Prophet's instruction, people will take the Antichrist's mark on their right hand or forehead. Satan will choose these places so that the mark will be clearly visible, but there is further significance to the placement of the mark. Again, Satan is copying God. God has instructed His people from the beginning to wear reminders of God on their hands and on their foreheads (Deuteronomy 6:4-9). We are to carry the Word of God with us daily, and in that way be marked by GOD. The Antichrist will want to erase reminders of God and instead plaster his name on people with this mark. Satan wants to place a brand on those he deceives. Satan will try to convince people that the Antichrist is really God, but the Antichrist pales in comparison to Jesus, the true God and Savior of our souls. God has already promised to write His name, the name of the New Jerusalem, and Jesus' new name on all His conquerors (Revelation 3:12). If we place our faith in Jesus, He will seal us, place His name on us, and prevent Satan from laying claim to us.

God wants us to know His Word because it is intimately connected to and leads to Him (John 1:1). If you carry the Word with you daily, you will be able to identify and avoid false teachers, and you will be marked by God, not Satan. When you receive salvation, God puts His name on you, and you are His. It doesn't matter to us what the Antichrist's name will be. We who believe in Jesus as God, our one and only Savior, will never be marked by the Antichrist's name. Make sure God's name is on you so that the Antichrist's name won't be. Bind God's Word on your hand, your head, and your heart, and carry Him with you everywhere you go.

Chapter Nine
The Seventh Seal and the
Trumpet Judgments
Revelation 8:1-9:21

There are three sets of judgments prophesied in Revelation. These are the seal, trumpet, and bowl judgments. Each set of judgments will consist of seven events, and the last event of the seal and trumpet judgments will contain the next set of judgments. We have already studied most of the seal judgments, but in this chapter, we will study the seventh seal and the trumpet judgments that it will release. The opening of the seventh seal will be one of the first events of the second half of the Tribulation, and the trumpet and bowl judgments will follow close behind.

When Jesus opens the seventh seal, there will be silence in heaven for half an hour. This is a marked difference from the tumultuous events of the first six seals. This silence is especially odd because we know that God is worshipped audibly in heaven at all times (Revelation 4:8-11). His praise never ceases. Yet when Jesus opens the seventh seal, the audible worship will stop. There will be absolute silence in heaven. This should clue us in to the severity and gravity of what is about to occur on the earth. As bad as the effects of the first six seals will be, this silence indicates that the wrath of God is about to be amped up. The seventh seal will initiate the seven trumpet judgments; when it is broken, seven angels who stand before God will be given seven trumpets that they will sound to signal the next set of judgments.

Before the trumpets sound, however, another angel will come to the altar before God with a golden censer. He will be given much incense to offer on the altar, along with the prayers of the saints that are already on the altar (Revelation 5:8). The angel with the censer will take fire from the altar, and he will pour that fire on the earth. The fire will come with rumblings, thunder, lightning, and an earthquake. These are all warning signs. When you hear thunder, see lightning, or feel the rumblings of an earthquake coming on, you run for shelter. These warnings are another opportunity for the people on earth during the Tribulation to turn to God. God is just and right in allowing the coming judgment (Revelation 16:5-7), but it will be devastating. God will send His judgment and His wrath on man for their sin, but He will be merciful and give opportunities for them to be saved all the way until the very end.

As the fire from the altar is thrown down to the earth, the seven angels will begin to blow their trumpets one by one. With the first trumpet, hail, fire, and blood will be thrown on the earth. One third of the earth will be burned by this mixture—a third of the trees will be burned, and all the green grass will be burnt up. It seems impossible that both hail and fire could exist at the same time. God will use these incongruous events to seize the world's attention.

The second trumpet will cause something like a flaming mountain, possibly a meteorite, to be thrown into the sea. This will turn one third of the ocean into blood, and it will kill one third of the sea animals and destroy one third of the ships in the sea. The third trumpet will cause a star to fall from heaven and hit the fresh water like a blazing torch. This star's name is Wormwood. Wormwood will turn one third of the earth's fresh water bitter, and many people will die because of the bitter water. God has sent this type of punishment before. Once He made the waters of Israel poisonous, in some translations, literally "wormwood," because they worshipped false gods (Jeremiah 9:12-16). He fed them wormwood, scattered them to all nations, and made their land a desolate waste. God is consistent and fair in His judgments. Because of the unfaithfulness and rebellion of the world during the Tribulation, God will again turn the waters to wormwood.

The fourth trumpet will affect the sun, moon, and stars in some way that will cause the day to lose one third of its light. The night will lose one third of its light as well. The Bible doesn't say exactly what astronomical event will cause the heavenly bodies to dim this way, but how it will happen does not matter. Jesus has promised us that it will, and that is good enough (Luke 21:25-28). At the fourth trumpet, the powers of the heavens will be shaken, and that is yet another signal for Israel that Jesus is coming back, and they should get ready.

After he saw the first four trumpets sound, John saw an eagle flying overhead and crying with a loud voice: "WOE, WOE, WOE," to those who dwell on the earth because of what will happen when the last three trumpets sound! We have seen a lot of destruction and judgment through the seals and the trumpets so far, but what is coming will be even worse. The judgment of the first four trumpets affected nature primarily, but the last three trumpets are three woes that will specifically target people.

The fifth angel will blow his trumpet to release the first woe. At this action, demons in the shape of locusts will be released from the bottomless pit. They will torture all humans that do not have the seal of God on their foreheads. These demons will torment people for five months, and they will inflict pain so great that their victims will wish to die, but they will not be able to. This passage says that the demon locusts will not be allowed to harm the green grass. This signifies that this judgment is aimed specifically toward humanity. It also shows that some time will pass between the first and fifth trumpets, because the green grass that will be burnt up at the first trumpet will have time to grow back before the fifth trumpet releases the demons.

These locust demons will come out of the bottomless pit, which is also called "the abyss." The abyss is a prison for demons. The angel that will be given the key to release the demons from prison is called Abaddon in Hebrew and Apollyon in Greek, and he rules over the demons. This 'Abaddon' or 'Apollyon' could be Satan, or he could just be a powerful fallen angel. The Bible doesn't tell us who he is, but we do know that everything he does is sanctioned and planned out by God. The keys to the abyss must be given to him; he does not have them in his possession. He has no power that God does not allow him. One day the abyss will imprison and torture Satan just as it does the demons; Satan does not rule over hell. Jesus holds the keys to death and Hades, not Satan or any fallen angel (Revelation 1:17-18). God is the warden of the abyss, and He lets the demons in and out according to His plans. These demons that will appear as locusts will only leave the pit when God allows it.

Joel spoke of this coming day. He warned of a coming army of locust that will have the appearance of horses, sound like chariots, and devour everything before them, causing people anguish (Joel 2:1-11). Even though they are demons, this plague is still called God's army because God will use them for His purpose and glory. The demons released by the fifth trumpet were bound by God, and He will oversee their temporary release.

The Bible clearly says that the only people that the locusts will not sting are those who have the seal of God on their foreheads. So, to find out who will avoid this woe, we must determine who will be sealed by God during the Tribulation. We know that the 144,000 will be sealed by God during the Tribulation (Revelation 7:3-4), but we do not know whether believers during the Tribulation Period will be marked like that. In fact, this is a topic of great debate. Some say that because these woes are God's punishment on the wicked, believers will not be attacked. On the other hand, we know all too well that salvation does not mean you will be spared from pain and trials. After all, God allowed Satan to physically afflict Job (Job 1:8-19, 2:1-7), and Paul was given an affliction from Satan (2 Corinthians 12:7-9), and both were righteous, godly men.

In this Church Age, the Holy Spirit comes to indwell those who believe in Jesus as Lord, and in that way, we are sealed by God (Ephesians 1:13-14). The restraining power of the Holy Spirit will leave the earth when the Church is raptured (2 Thessalonians 2:7), and because of that departure I do not think that God will seal Tribulation believers during their time on earth. I believe the scriptures indicate that only those who endure until the end, whether they are martyred for their faith or survive until Jesus returns to defeat His enemies, will finally be saved and sealed by God (Matthew 24:9-13). Believers that come out of the Tribulation will have their tears wiped away, but they will not avoid suffering during the Tribulation. They will hunger and thirst, and they will be scorched by the sun (Revelation 7:13-17). The Bible is clear that believers in the Tribulation will not escape trial. Why would this trumpet judgment be any different?

Believers are not promised protection from pain, except for the 144,000 (Revelation 7:3, 9:4). I believe that the 144,000 will be the only people sealed by God in the Tribulation, and thus I think that the locust demons will sting Tribulation believers. God could choose to seal the believers in the Tribulation as well, but the 144,000 are the only people that scripture clearly says will be marked by God in the Tribulation. Whichever way God chooses to do it, He is holy and right and just. Do not choose what you believe based on what you would prefer; believe what the scriptures say.

The second woe will begin when the sixth trumpet is blown. When this trumpet sounds, four angels that are bound at the river Euphrates will be released to kill one third of mankind. The fact that these angels are bound indicates that they are not good angels; they fell with Satan, and God bound them. They are poised for attack; they have not been released yet, but they are at attention, waiting to be loosed. When they are released, they will lead an army of two hundred million troops. The Bible is clear that this is not a human army. The army's horses will have lions' heads, wound people with tails that are like serpents, and they will breathe fire, smoke, and sulfur. These emissions will kill another third of mankind, in addition to the fourth killed by the four horsemen. These troops are demons, not people. This army will attack all peoples on earth; no people group will lead the attack.

It is significant that the fallen angels are bound at the river Euphrates. God originally gave Israel all the land from the Nile River to the River Euphrates as their inheritance (Genesis 15:18-21). The river Euphrates was the northernmost boundary of the land that God gave to Abraham and Israel. The land that we now recognize as Israel is nowhere near as big as what God originally gave them. At Jesus' second coming, God will complete His promise and Israel will receive all the land that He has set apart for them. The true bounds of Israel will include modern day Lebanon, Jordan, and most of Syria. Jesus will return to reign over His physical kingdom, and Abraham, Isaac, and Jacob will reign with Him, finally receiving the land that Jesus promised to them (Hebrews 11:8-16).

Even after the events of the first two woes, which will be clear judgments from God, mankind will not repent of their sins or give up their idolatry. They will not be ignorant; they will know that God is working, but their hearts will be hardened to the truth. It is extremely dangerous to willfully harden your heart. As an unbeliever, if you repeatedly harden your heart to God's drawing and the opportunities that He gives you to repent, God will eventually harden your heart permanently so that you cannot be saved (John 12:37-40). This point is different for each person and will only come after someone has hardened their own heart first. God gave us a clear example of this process in Pharaoh. God stated from the beginning of the process that He would harden Pharaoh's heart, because He knew the choices that Pharaoh would make. You can trace the pattern of Pharaoh hardening his heart over and over (Exodus 7:1-23, 8:15-32, 9:7) until God gave him a taste of a permanently hardened heart (Exodus 9:12). God gave Pharaoh one more chance (Exodus 9:34-35), but when Pharaoh still refused God's mercy, God permanently hardened Pharaoh's heart (Exodus 10:1-2, 20, 27, 11:9-10).

Those left at this point in the Tribulation will have the attitude of Pharaoh. After all of God's signs and all their opportunities to repent, they will still harden their hearts to God. Because of this, God will send a strong delusion upon them that will make it difficult for them to believe and eventually take the final measure of hardening their hearts against Him (2 Thessalonians 2:11-12). Believe in Jesus now so that you do not find yourself in that position. They will see the error of their ways when their hardened hearts cause them to be separated from God and punished for eternity.

Chapter Ten
A Break in Prophesying, the Seventh Trumpet, and the Bowl Judgments
Revelation 10, 11:15-19, 15, and 16

•••

A Break in Prophesying
Revelation 10:1-11

Before John recorded the events of the seventh trumpet and the seven bowl judgments that it will contain, God gave him a vision of an angel coming down from heaven. This angel called out, and the seven thunders responded. God did not allow John to record what the thunders said. He wanted John to take a break from prophesying. Then the angel declared that the mystery of God would quickly be fully revealed, and after John ate a little scroll from the angel's hand he was told to prophesy again. These events were an interlude before John recorded the events of the seventh trumpet and the rest of the Tribulation.

This mighty angel that descended from heaven was wrapped in a cloud. He had a rainbow over his head, legs like pillars of fire, and the voice of a roaring lion. The similarity of these attributes to the imagery associated with God has caused many to think that this figure is Jesus, but he isn't. He is just an immensely powerful angel. We know that this angel is not Jesus because he is described as *another* mighty angel. There was a mighty angel described earlier in Revelation (Revelation 5:2), which is why scripture describes this angel as *another*. This angel cannot be Jesus. Jesus is God; He cannot be described as *another* because there is no one like Him. The angel has traits like God's simply because he is a very holy, powerful, and important angel.

When this mighty angel spoke, the seven thunders responded. After they finished speaking, John started to write down what they had said, but God stopped him. It has been popular in the faith community to guess at what the thunders said, but this passage makes it clear that we are not supposed to know! John wrote the message of Revelation for us, the Church (Revelation 1:1). If John wasn't allowed to write down what the thunders said, it is because the message was not for us. God knows things that we don't, but He tells us what we need to know (Deuteronomy 29:29). God's glory increases when He conceals things from us. God is not God if He doesn't know more than we do, so if He doesn't want you to know something, trust that He knows best!

After the thunders finished speaking, the angel swore by God that there would be no more delay; the mystery of God would be fulfilled in the days of the seventh trumpet. That doesn't mean that the seventh trumpet is the last event of the Tribulation; just that everything else that must happen in the Tribulation (e.g., the seven bowl judgments and the Battle of Armageddon) will happen very quickly after the trumpet is blown, likely within days. These events will reveal the complete mystery of God. The "mystery of God" is all the prophecies God has given us about the end times and His eternal rule. In the days of the last trumpet, they will all be fulfilled and make sense.

This mystery was announced to the Old Testament prophets—God gave the original prophecies to them. God did not always reveal the meanings of these prophecies to the prophets, but they knew that the message was important, so they recorded them for us (1 Peter 1:10-12). Since the days of the Old Testament, many prophecies have been fulfilled and we have been given some new prophecies, including parts of this Revelation of John. As we have demonstrated, much of Revelation simply points to prophecies in the Old Testament, but some prophecies in Revelation are new. Because of these new revelations, we understand the 'mystery' a little bit better than the prophets did, but God still has not revealed the complete mystery to us. Since we in the Church will not be here during the Tribulation Period to see the final fulfillment of prophecy, we have the same responsibility that the Old Testament prophets did: to proclaim what God has revealed to us. We are in the end times, and many prophecies that were not revealed to the Old Testament prophets are ripe for interpretation now (Daniel 12:4-10, Revelation 22:10).

After the angel's announcement, God told John to go and take a little scroll out of the hand of the mighty angel. When he did, the angel told John to eat the scroll, and he warned that it would taste sweet but be bitter in John's stomach. Something like this has happened before in the Bible. Ezekiel once ate a scroll of woe that tasted sweet as honey and then went to Israel to prophesy the Word that God had given him (Ezekiel 2:8-3:7). John was also given a Word from God to preach to all the nations. Both messages were of judgment, mourning, and woe. John's scroll was sweet on his tongue because he knew that his salvation had saved him from these prophecies. It turned bitter in his stomach because he ached for those who do not believe. The Word is sweet to us who know God through Jesus and are spared His wrath (Psalm 119:103, Jeremiah 15:16), but we hurt for those who reject God's Word.

The days are short, and God has given us a message to share. Study the message and pray for understanding so that you can share it with others. John faithfully passed on God's words to the Church, and the Church has been told to share that message with the lost, so that the lost might be able to recognize what is happening when the Tribulation judgments begin. There are still more Tribulation events to study and pass on. After John ate this scroll that represented the Words of God, he was told that he must again prophesy about many things. There is judgment still to come: the seventh trumpet, and the seven bowl judgments.

•••

The Seventh Trumpet
Revelation 11:15-19, 15:1-8

The seventh trumpet will introduce the last of the three woes that were declared after John's vision of the fourth trumpet (Revelation 8:13). This woe will consist of seven bowls or plagues of God's wrath that will be poured out on the earth. There will be no more delays in God accomplishing His purposes once the seventh trumpet has been blown. The bowls of judgment will be poured out very quickly, even simultaneously, because they must be poured out to set the stage for Jesus' return to earth. Once the bowl judgments are complete, Jesus will return to defeat His enemies and set up His literal kingdom on the earth.

Jesus <u>must</u> return to set up His Millennial Kingdom on this earth. Daniel prophesied that Jesus would be given the kingdoms of *this world* (Daniel 7:13-14). Additionally, earlier in Daniel's life, Daniel saw that the stone not cut by human hands (Jesus) will destroy the last remaining physical kingdom and set up his own physical kingdom (Daniel 2:31-35, 44-45). Jesus' kingdom is not only spiritual. When He comes again, Jesus' kingdom will fill the whole earth! The seventh trumpet will set the stage for the culmination of this eternal plan. When the seventh trumpet is blown, voices from heaven will declare that the world is now the kingdom of the Lord Jesus Christ, because

He has begun to visibly exercise His eternal authority over the world.

When the seventh trumpet sounds, Jesus will begin to reign. He will not have physically set foot on the earth to rule yet, but at the sounding of the seventh trumpet in the Tribulation Period, God is no longer described as "to come." He is only described as "who *is* and who was" because at that point, *He will have already begun to reign* (Revelation 16:5, 11:17)! When the seventh trumpet blows, He will not be yet to come, He will be present! Jesus' thousand-year reign will begin at the seventh trumpet, before He has even set foot on the earth, and as the Tribulation draws to a close, Jesus will begin to exercise the power that He has always possessed.

Jesus will begin to rule at the seventh trumpet, but the people that are left on earth will not worship or obey Him as Lord and King. At the beginning of the Tribulation Period, people will be afraid of God's judgment, and they will call on the mountains to hide them from God's wrath (Revelation 6:15-17). By the time of the seventh trumpet and the bowls, the nations will rage against God and resist His rule (Revelation 11:18). The nations that will assemble for battle in the valley of Armageddon will not necessarily be gathering against Israel; they will gather to fight against Jesus, the Anointed One (Psalm 2:1-3). This is not surprising given that the armies will be gathered by the unholy trinity and demons (Revelation 16:13-14). Mankind will defy God to the very end, so God will complete His judgment of the earth and its inhabitants.

Just as the seventh seal will contain the seven trumpets, the seventh trumpet will contain the seven plagues of the bowls (Revelation 11:15-19, 15:1-8, 10:5-7). In the days of the seventh trumpet, seven angels will be given bowls of God's wrath, and they will pour the plagues out on the earth to complete God's judgment. Before John saw the angels emerge in his vision, however, he saw a vision of a crowd of believers who will be killed because they won't take the mark of the beast or worship its image. John saw these believers standing around a sea of glass mingled with fire. They held harps and sang two songs: The Song of Moses and the Song of the Lamb. John doesn't explain the significance or full content of these songs in this passage, so that indicates that these songs have appeared elsewhere in scripture.

After God delivered the Israelites from the brutal control of Pharaoh, the nation of Israel sang a beautiful song of deliverance and praise to God because He defeated their enemies (Exodus 15:1-18). Many think that this is the Song of Moses that the martyrs are singing in our passage, but there is another Song of Moses that I believe matches the context of the martyrs' worship better. In this other Song of Moses, God laid out Israel's entire history for them. The culmination of this song is a declaration that God will avenge His people, take vengeance on His adversaries, and cleanse the land (Deuteronomy 31:30-32:43). This is exactly what God is preparing to do in the context of the seventh trumpet, and so I believe that this is the Song of Moses that the martyrs will sing around the sea of glass and fire.

The other song the martyrs will sing is the Song of the Lamb, which we have already seen in Revelation (Revelation 5:8-14). Both the Song of Moses and the Song of the Lamb declare that God is good and right in all that He does because He has planned everything out from the beginning. That message is reflected in the snippet of song that John records in this passage. Jesus will reign because He is worthy, and all believers will continue to praise God as the kingdoms of this world become the kingdom of our Lord and of His Christ. He shall reign forever and ever, and heaven will be on the earth as God dwells with us forever.

When the time is right, Jesus will receive worship, praise, and a kingdom that will never end! When He sets up His kingdom on the earth, everyone will acknowledge that He is the Lord (Philippians 2:9-11). He will unite all things under Himself (Ephesians 1:7-10), and His kingdom will have no end (Hebrews 1:8-12). Jesus is coming back to this earth, just as surely as He came the first time. Become a part of His Kingdom today, and you will get to experience the joys of the Millennial Kingdom when Jesus returns to this earth!

●●●

The Bowl Judgments
Revelation 16:1-21

After Jesus begins to reign and the seven angels holding plagues have received the bowls of God's wrath, God will command these angels to pour their bowls out onto the earth. The bowl plagues will devastate the earth and punish mankind for their rebellion against God. The first bowl will bring sores on all the worshipers of the beast. The second will turn all the sea into blood. Earlier in the Tribulation Period, at the second trumpet, one third of the sea will become blood; at this second bowl, *all* the oceans will become blood. The waters will be like the blood of a corpse; coagulated and malodorous. The third bowl will turn all fresh waters to blood as well. Rapidly, the landscape of earth will become uninhabitable. These bowls must be poured out quickly; if God did not shorten these days of judgment, no one would remain alive (Matthew 24:21-22).

At the fourth bowl, the sun will scorch the people of the earth with fire, and still, they will not repent of their ways. Instead, they will curse God. The world's obstinate, sinful attitude towards God that we saw foretold at the seventh trumpet will persist. Then God will have the fifth angel pour darkness onto the throne and kingdom of the beast, which is Babylon. Zechariah prophesied that the seat of all wickedness would be in Shinar, which means Babylon (Zechariah 5:5-11). Everything else in that passage is symbolic and God explains what it means; but there was no metaphor for the place that wickedness was being taken, because they said clearly that she was being taken to Babylon. The Antichrist's kingdom will be based in Babylon and extend to all the other places that the one world government will rule, and these will all be plunged into darkness by the fifth bowl. God will begin the destruction of Babylon with the fifth bowl judgment.

When the sixth bowl is poured out, the river Euphrates will dry up. Also at this bowl, John saw something like frogs coming from the mouths of the False Prophet, the Antichrist, and Satan. These frogs are demonic spirits that will tempt the kings of the world to assemble and get ready to fight Jesus. The kings from the east will travel through the bed of the dry Euphrates, and all the kings and their armies will assemble at Armageddon. Soon God will reap the harvest of the earth at the Battle of Armageddon, and the blood from this battle will fill the valley of Megiddo (Revelation 14:14-20).

The seventh and last bowl of judgment will be poured into the air, and there will be an earthquake so great that all nations will fall, all islands will disappear, and every mountain around the globe will be leveled. There will no longer be mountains for people to call on to hide them from God's wrath (Revelation 6:15-17). Instead, 100-pound hailstones will fall from the heavens and crush people because they will remain unrepentant. They will continue to rage against God. Babylon will receive a special outpouring of God's wrath at this time. This earthquake will also split the city of Jerusalem into three parts, but it will not destroy it. The rest of the world will be decimated, but the split of Jerusalem will prepare it for the Millennial Kingdom. When Jesus comes back, Jerusalem will be set up as the seat of His power. At this last bowl, Jerusalem will be divided into northern, middle, and southern sections, and the middle section, where the temple mount is, will be raised above the rest of the city (Zechariah 14:4-11, Micah 4:1-2).

Amid John's visions of the Tribulation judgments, Jesus showed him the Ark of the Covenant in the temple (Revelation 11:19). The Ark of the Covenant is a reminder of God's faithfulness to Israel. It reminds His people of His presence with them, His atonement for them, and His covenant with them. Because the Jews rejected Jesus as their Messiah, God placed their covenant on hold, but He will be faithful to complete it. The Tribulation will refine the Jews by fire like silver and gold, but this vision of the Ark shows that God has not forgotten about them. After the Rapture, God will return His focus to the Jews and resume the process of fulfilling His covenant with them. That is why John wrote that Jesus said "Behold, I come like a thief" in the context of the last judgments. He knew that the unbelieving Jews might not be looking for the Messiah's return. John was reminding the Jews of Jesus' teaching from the Olivet discourse, and how Jesus had tried to prepare them for His unexpected return (Revelation 16:15, Matthew 24:42-44).

In the Olivet discourse, Jesus warned believers in the Tribulation, especially the Jews, not to be like those who are asleep. At this point in the Tribulation, Jesus will have already come to get His Church and He will have already begun to reign through bringing the judgments on the earth, but He will not yet have returned physically and permanently. He will still surprise many when He does because they will not understand the truth of the Bible. That is exactly why John echoed Jesus' instructions: when the nations of the world gather to fight against God, Israel should *stay awake*! Jesus is coming soon, like a thief in the night.

Paul had to remind the Thessalonians that the thief in the night was something that only those *in the night* needed to fear (1 Thessalonians 5:1-6). Those who have faith in God through Jesus Christ are people of the day, and we will not be surprised by Jesus' return for us, whether we are Church Age believers who await the Rapture or Tribulation Believers who await Jesus' physical return to the earth. If you are awake when the thief comes, you will not be taken by surprise. Anyone who is not a child of light will be "asleep" or unaware when Jesus returns, whether at the Rapture or the return. When God's wrath comes, it will all happen quickly, so believe in Jesus' name and *stay awake*, lest you are surprised by the thief.

Chapter Eleven
The Religious and Economic Destruction of Babylon
Revelation 17-18

During the Tribulation, the headquarters of the one world government and the Antichrist's reign will be in Babylon. That city will once again be a powerful and influential city, but God will bring judgment upon it during the seventh bowl judgment. In this chapter we will delve further into the destruction of Babylon that was mentioned during our study of the bowls. Revelation describes two aspects of Babylon's destruction: its spiritual judgment and its economic downfall. During the Tribulation, Babylon will be judged both for its religious idolatry and its material and commercial sins. Babylon was once the root of organized false religion, and during the Tribulation Period, another false religion will spread from there.

There are many people who do not believe that Babylon will be the seat of the world's power during the Tribulation. They think the woman in this passage is just named 'Babylon' figuratively, and she simply signifies a wicked city. None of the reasons for this belief are based on what the scripture says. The scripture says that the one world government will be based in Babylon (Revelation 17:5&18), and as we have seen via the various prophecies we have studied, God's Word speaks literally unless it is explained to be symbolism. Simply put, if the Bible says that Babylon will be the headquarters of everything that happens in the last days, believe it. Nevertheless, let's explore why some don't believe Babylon to be the powerful city that Revelation talks about.

Some people think that instead of Babylon, the one world government will be based in Rome. They get this idea from the fact that the seven heads of the beast that the woman sits on partially refer to seven hills, and Rome is referred to as the city on seven hills. There are many cities on earth that sit on seven hills. To assume that the false religion will be based in Rome because of this one phrase is irresponsible. Some say that the Bible cannot mean Babylon because Babylon no longer exists. Do not limit God in that way! If He says that the center of false religion and the seat of the Antichrist's power will be Babylon, He can make the city prosper again!

Still, some people reject Babylon as the seat of power because Babylon isn't in what we perceive to be a powerful location. It is in a desert and does not seem like it has the potential to be a world power. All these objections come from human limitations and logic. If God wants to, He can raise Babylon to be an influential city again. The stage is already being set for its reemergence—Babylon is being rebuilt, the United States of America has built a grand embassy right nearby in Baghdad, and the oil industry is beginning to boom in that area. At some point, the headquarters of the world will be in Babylon. It may take some time, but we are getting closer to that reality every day. The Rapture could happen before power has moved to Babylon, but just know that when the Tribulation Period begins, the world's seat of power will be Babylon.

As a world power, Babylon is accused of committing sexual immorality with the kings of the earth (Revelation 17:1-2, 14:8). This seems confusing; how can a city commit sexual immorality? Sexual immorality in this context refers to the spiritual unfaithfulness of the city's inhabitants and leaders. God is a jealous God, and He wants to be the only one that we worship. Worship of any other kind is idolatry, and He sees it as adultery (Deuteronomy 6:14-15, Exodus 34:13-17). We are to have no other gods before God (Exodus 20:1-6). When we are enticed by and go after the world, God considers that unfaithfulness (James 4:4-5). So, when our passage talks about the woman committing sexual immorality with the kings of the earth, it is referring to how Babylon and its leaders have taught the kings of the world to worship other things besides the one true God. Babylon has this type of influence because all organized false religion stems from Babylon.

There has always been a temptation to sin, and Adam and Eve deciding to listen to Satan instead of God in the Garden of Eden was the first instance of unfaithfulness to God. But organized false religion has its root in Babylon, a place that God originally called Babel (Genesis 11:1-9). Nimrod founded civilization in Shinar, an area that would eventually include Babylon (Genesis 10:6-10). False worship began with a false god named Tammuz, who many believe was descended from Nimrod. The tradition around Tammuz taught that he died and came back to life;[8] Tammuz is an early example of Satan trying to copy God by mimicking Jesus' death and resurrection. The Jews even fell prey to false worship of Tammuz, and God loathed it (Ezekiel 8:1-18). This organized unfaithfulness led to other forms of disobedience to God.

At Babel, people decided that they did not want to spread across the whole earth, as God had commanded them to do (Genesis 1:26-28, 9:1). They were prideful and wanted to make a name for themselves, and so they started building a tower to the heavens. This was sinful for many reasons. They were blatantly disobedient to God, arrogant, and focused on their own glory. We are not supposed to focus on making a name for ourselves. We are to contribute to the glory of God. We are to search out what God would have us do and where He would have us go, and then do that. When God saw what

---

[8] MacArthur, John. *The MacArthur Bible Commentary*. Thomas Nelson, 2005.

the Babylonians were doing, He acknowledged that they could do anything if they continued to speak the same language and work together. Therefore, God scattered them for their pride and insolence, and He confused their speech to keep them humble.

As time goes on, our culture is trying to return to one language and government, just like the people of Babel. With translators and agreements between countries, we try to form alliances that will make us the most powerful. While these seem like positive things, they will lead to arrogance and cause people to think we don't need God. Organized unfaithfulness started with the Babylonians' perceived independence from the true God, and it will end the same way. At the right time, the seat of wickedness (the coming one-world government) will move back to Babylon (Zechariah 5:5-11). Scripture clearly indicates that this government will implement one standardized religion, and God will then bring His final judgment on this world as the new Babylon echoes the original arrogance of the Tower of Babel.

The woman (Babylon, and the one world false religion) will sit on the beast for a time. Remember, this beast is the Antichrist and his kingdom (Revelation 17:8-11). The seven heads of this beast represent seven world kingdoms. At the time of John's writing, five of those kingdoms had fallen. Those kingdoms were Egypt, Assyria, Babylon, Medo-Persia, and Greece. At the time that Revelation was written, one of those seven kingdoms was still reigning (Rome), and one kingdom is yet to come even now. All we know about this kingdom that is still coming is that it will be made up of ten world powers. The Bible does not state exactly which ones. That kingdom will only last for a short while, and then the kings will hand over their power to the Antichrist. The Antichrist's kingdom will be an eighth kingdom that will be formed out of the seventh kingdom.

This one world religion and government will attempt to kill all people who are faithful to Jesus and believe that He is the only way to be saved. The Church will be gone, but any people who come to faith and manage to avoid this false religion that will spread across the world will be put to death for not joining the one world religion. We do not know what this world religion will be, but it will be pervasive and deceptive. This false religion will be powerful, and it will have enough influence to martyr anyone who holds to the truth (Revelation 17:6, 18:24). The Antichrist will support this religion for the first half of his reign.

At the midpoint of the Tribulation Period, however, the Antichrist will turn on this religion, declare himself to be god, and proclaim that people should only worship him. The Antichrist, the False Prophet, and their kingdom will destroy the world religion and create a new one with the Antichrist at its center (2 Thessalonians 2:3-4). Daniel received a prophecy about four world kingdoms that stated that the Antichrist will put down three of the ten leaders of the final world kingdom and "change the times and the law" (Daniel 7:1-8, 15-28). He will change the times and the law when he casts down the world religion and makes himself out to be god. From then on, only worship of the Antichrist himself will be allowed.

Babylon's future has been decreed from the beginning; most of Revelation chapter eighteen consists of direct quotes from Old Testament prophecy. John under the leadership of the Spirit recorded exactly how the end times will occur, and his prophecies match up to Old Testament prophecy. Compare Revelation 18:4-6, 21-24 to Jeremiah 51:45-64, and compare Revelation 18:7-8 to Isaiah 47:7-9. John saw visions of the clear fulfillment of prophecies about a future destruction of Babylon. The prophecies he quoted cannot refer only to Babylon's destruction at the hands of the Medo-Persians; at John's time, the destruction by the Medo-Persians had already occurred.

John quoted those prophecies anew to remind us that their complete fulfillment is yet future. Babylon must rise again so that it can go to destruction.

Babylon will be the headquarters of civilization in the end times, but because of its religious idolatry and material and commercial sins, God will destroy it (Isaiah 13:1-13, 19-22). A prophecy in Isaiah thirteen describes the destruction of the Battle of Armageddon and the effects of God's final judgment (Isaiah 13:1-13), then it describes the sacking of Babylon by the Medo-Persians (v. 14-18), and then it jumps ahead again to the results of God's final judgment (v. 19-22). God has already brought some judgment on Babylon through the Medes and the Persians, but their sacking of Babylon did not include everything talked about in Isaiah's full prophecy. Babylon may be abandoned now, but the prophecies about Babylon never being inhabited again because of its destruction have not been fulfilled yet. The Medo-Persians lived in Babylon after their attack, and archaeologists are returning to restore Babylon; therefore, there must still be judgment to come for Babylon (Isaiah 14:22-23, Jeremiah 50:13).

For Babylon to be destroyed again, it must be rebuilt and inhabited again. Then, after it is restored to its former greatness, God will bring His judgment on it. In the midst of God shaking the earth and the heavens, at the seventh bowl, God will pour out His wrath on Babylon (Revelation 16:16-19). This destruction described in many prophecies cannot be carried out by man, because God declares that He will do it (Isaiah 13:3-6, 9-14, 14:22-23, Jeremiah 51:36-43). That will be the destruction that Babylon cannot come back from. But before God destroys Babylon for the last time, it will have another moment of false glory and power, and it will again be the root of organized unfaithfulness and idolatry.

Do not be surprised as the power of the world shifts back towards that wickedness; it is what God has planned, and

He is in control of every rise to and fall from power. Yes, pray for your country. Pray for your leadership. Be active in your community. But above all else, share the Gospel in order to save souls. Don't get discouraged when the country and the world don't look the way you want them to. Studying Revelation should bring you peace, because it reminds us that the world is not as out of control as it seems. God has planned everything in advance. Thank God that we do not look to man or an earthly kingdom to take care of us. God has not lost His authority, and He is in control of the leaders of this world, whether we like them or not. Amid the craziness, He is what gives us a future and a hope (Jeremiah 29:11).

There is a final, righteous kingdom that is coming. It is already in us and among those who trust in Jesus, and He has told us what is going to happen. Because of the light that we have received, it is our responsibility to tell others what is coming next. Keep being salt and light until God takes us out of this world, because God is still restraining the man of lawlessness through the power of the Spirit that lives within each of us. Until He takes us away, we must stand for truth, preach righteousness, and at the same time love people. Take your eyes off the news and put them on the coming eternal kingdom. We cannot stop the direction of the world and we should not want to, because it is God's plan. But we should not just hide away and wait for Jesus' return, either (though we should be looking for it). If the salt of the earth loses its saltiness, it is of no use. Allow God to use His Spirit within you to slow the decay of wickedness on this world. The longer God waits to begin His final judgment, the more people will have the opportunity to receive salvation, and that is why we are still here.

Chapter Twelve
The Second Coming
Revelation 19:1-5, 11-21; 14:14-20

When the judgments of the Tribulation are complete, it will finally be time for the physical return of Jesus Christ to the earth! This is the culmination of the Tribulation Period. Babylon will have been destroyed, and while a great multitude is still praising God for the destruction of Babylon, Jesus will return physically to the earth and the Battle of Armageddon will commence. Studying Revelation in chronological order can be tricky because a lot of the things that must happen during the end times will happen all at the same time. It can be difficult to place certain things in true order because they will occur right on top of one another. The things we will study in this chapter will all happen at the same time. The destruction of Babylon and Jesus' simultaneous return will put many moving pieces into motion. As Jesus is coming back, many things will happen, including the harvest of the earth and the judgment of the nations via the Battle of Armageddon.

The great host in heaven that praise God for His judgments on both Babylon and the world are not rejoicing over the death of the wicked. God would not allow that because He does not want anyone to die; He wants all people to turn to Him and live (Ezekiel 18:23, 32). The rejoicing of the multitude will not be because the wicked are getting what they deserve, it will be because God is just and true and He keeps His promises. The word 'hallelujah' is only in the Bible four times, and all four uses are in the first six verses of Revelation chapter nineteen. This new form of worship is inspired by the righteousness and justice of Christ's judgment. This judgment has been prophesied for a long time. Every victim of God's judgment will be someone who rejected Jesus' offer of salvation. God promised that there would be consequences for rejecting Him as Savior (Matthew 7:21-23, Mark 3:28-29, Hebrews 10:26-31). All the bloodshed is the result of a just God keeping His promises. Jesus will completely fulfill all the prophecies about His second coming, just as He fulfilled the prophecies about His first coming.

There will be celebration when Jesus returns, but that day will primarily be a day of judgment. When Jesus came the first time, He came to bring good news, just as He said when preaching in the synagogue in Nazareth (Luke 4:16-21). When preaching in the synagogue, He stopped short of quoting the entire prophecy, because the second part of the prophecy referred to His second coming (Isaiah 61:1-2). Jesus' first coming was about salvation and grace, and His second will be about justice and vengeance. At His second coming, He will fulfill the second half of Isaiah's prophecy and it will be time for God's vengeance.

It is important to recognize how God works in different times so that you can rightly divide the Word of God and recognize which prophecies have been fulfilled and which have not yet been fulfilled (2 Timothy 2:15 KJV). This knowledge is crucial to recognizing passages like this one, where the Messiah's first coming and the Messiah's second are described in the same verse (Isaiah 61:2). When you study prophecy, you cannot assume that it will describe events in order or that a prophecy will only refer to one event. Prophecy jumps around, which is why as you study Revelation, you cannot assume that everything will occur in the order that John wrote it down! We must have eyes to see and ears to hear, and we must use the guidance of the Spirit to discern what event a prophecy is talking about.

God has fixed a day when He will judge the world, and He has appointed Jesus to be the Judge (Acts 17:29-31). God the Father judges no one, but Jesus the Son judges each person according to whether they have a relationship with Him (John 5:22, Matthew 7:21-23). Anyone who does not have a personal relationship with Jesus will be turned away from the Millennial Kingdom on the day of judgment. Although we do not know when that day will be, God does. It is already set. God already has a perfect plan in place, and every minute we edge closer to the day when Jesus will set foot on the earth to mete out judgment. The Day of Judgment has long been prophesied (Isaiah 2:12-17, 2 Peter 2:9). It will not be a fun day for the world or the nation of Israel; they will not escape the wrath and the woe (Jeremiah 30:1-11). We Church Age believers will only have relief from that day of judgment by grace alone through faith in Jesus Christ (1 Thessalonians 1:10, 5:9, Revelation 3:10). That day will be a day of terror from which mankind will not escape, but while God is meting out judgment the great multitude (the saints) will praise Him because His judgments will be just and right.

When Jesus returns, He will ride in on a white horse (Revelation 19:11-16). We have seen that the Antichrist will try to imitate this arrival at the breaking of the first seal (Revelation 6:1-2), but when Jesus comes back for real, there will be no denying that it is Him. There is no question who the scripture is describing. He has a sword coming out of His mouth (Revelation 1:16). He is named the King of Kings and Lord of Lords (Revelation 17:14, 1 Timothy 6:15, Deuteronomy 10:17). He will rule with an iron rod (Psalm 2:9), and His name is the Word of God (John 1:1). There is no doubt that this figure is Jesus. A multitude will come with Him, dressed in white. That's us! Jesus will be stained by the blood of His enemies, but the multitude will not be touched by the blood. Jesus will fight His battles upon His return; He doesn't need us to help (Isaiah 63:1-6).

All the nations of the earth will gather in the valley of Megiddo at the end of the Tribulation, after the trumpets and bowls are complete. Remember, they will not be gathered to fight against Israel. Israel will be scattered. Two-thirds of Israel will have been killed. Some of them will be in the wilderness in Bozrah, and some will remain in Jerusalem. Israel at this point will be under attack by the Antichrist; they won't be able to face an army. Instead, Satan will gather this army to fight against Jesus. Satan knows that Jesus is coming back to earth to set up His kingdom, and Satan isn't just going to hand the victory over to Him. There will be a massive battle on the earth when Jesus comes back.

When Jesus returns, He will come on a cloud to reap the harvest of the earth, and to tread the winepress of His wrath (Revelation 14:14-20). Daniel and Matthew both echo this image of Jesus coming on a cloud to receive His kingdom (Daniel 7:13-14, Matthew 24:29-31). When Jesus returns, He will gather His people from the four corners of the earth, but He will also put in His sickle to reap the unrighteous for judgment (Matthew 24:31, Revelation 14:14-16). The Revelation passage describes two harvests. First, Jesus will swing His sickle and harvest the earth. With this harvest, He will defeat His enemies by His own hand and get the earth ready for His Kingdom.

An angel will perform the action of the second harvest, under God's authority. This angel will come and gather the 'grapes' from the earth and place them in a winepress of God's wrath. These 'grapes' are the unrighteous people that will reject salvation until the very end. The winepress that they will enter will be trodden outside the city, and instead of grape juice, blood will flow out of it. So much blood will come out of this press that it will pool as deep as a horse's bridle and 1600 stadia long. The Battle of Armageddon is the winepress of God's wrath, and those who will gather to fight against Jesus are the 'grapes' that will be trodden in it. The battle will wage outside of Jerusalem, from Armageddon to Edom.[9] The nations of the earth will gather in the valley of Megiddo, and God will be there to deal with them (Joel 3:9-16).

At the end of the age, Jesus' angels will gather the wicked and cast them into the winepress, and members of God's Kingdom will be left behind to reside peacefully in the Millennial Kingdom (Matthew 13:24-30, 36-43). The kingdom of God does exist now, reigning in the hearts and lives of those who have His Spirit within us, because He is King of Kings and Lord of Lords over our lives. Yet, the world right now is not His Kingdom. God is allowing Satan to have dominion over the earth for a time. There is still a time to come when God will exercise His true authority over the world, and it will become His physical Kingdom. Too many Christians say that there is no future physical Millennial Kingdom; that the Church Age is the only Kingdom the Bible speaks of. They are wrong. Scripture that was written during the Church Age says that there is still a *coming* Kingdom (Matthew 6:9-10). After the harvest, when the wicked are taken away and the righteous are left, God will finally claim His earth. Then, the righteous will shine in the Kingdom. God's physical Kingdom is yet to come.

During the harvests, the scripture says that the Lord will have a sacrifice in Bozrah (Isaiah 34:1-6). Bozrah is a place in Edom, southeast of Jerusalem. I believe without question that the sacrifice mentioned in that passage is the nation of Israel, and that Bozrah is where the Israelites will run to when the Antichrist chases them out of Jerusalem at the midpoint of the Tribulation. That is where God will shelter and protect them for three and a half years. Additionally, I believe that is where Jesus will first set foot when He returns to earth.

---

[9] MacArthur, John. *The MacArthur Bible Commentary*. Thomas Nelson, 2005.

For years I believed that Jesus would return first to the Mount of Olives. I just assumed that He would return not only in the same manner that He left, as the angel said (Acts 1:10-11), but also to the same place that He left. I also believed this because of a prophecy about the Mount of Olives splitting in two when Jesus steps onto it (Zechariah 14:3-4). Jesus will set foot on the Mount of Olives, and it will split in two, but that is not where He will set foot *first*. The scripture shows us that He will return first to His people in Bozrah (Isaiah 63:1). Then He will defeat His enemies in the battle of Armageddon as He travels all the way to Jerusalem, and there He will step onto the Mount of Olives. On this journey, Jesus will lead the Israelites out from Bozrah (Micah 2:12-13 ASV & KJV), and He will be stained in blood from the winepress of His wrath, but His sheep will be dressed in garments white as snow. Jesus is the only one doing the fighting in this battle. The nations will gather against Him, and Satan will have convinced them that they are going to win, but Jesus will defeat them all by Himself.

There is a battle prophesied in Ezekiel chapters thirty-eight and thirty-nine, the battle of Gog and Magog, that I believe will culminate in the battle of Armageddon. Many Bible teachers that I respect teach that this battle will occur before the Tribulation begins, but I believe the scripture teaches that it will begin at the midpoint of the Tribulation and culminate with the Battle of Armageddon at Jesus' return. The main argument for Gog and Magog happening before the Tribulation is a scripture that says the spoils from the battle will be gathered for seven years afterward (Ezekiel 39:9-10), and so those who teach it claim that means that the spoils will be gathered throughout the seven-year Tribulation. One, that is a big assumption. Two, I don't believe that people will be concerned with collecting spoils, especially during the second half of the Tribulation. They will be too concerned with staying alive. The scripture says that Gog and Magog will attack Israel during a time of peace (Ezekiel 38:14-16). That peace will not be possible prior to the Tribulation. It will only come when they sign that treaty with the Antichrist and are lulled into a false sense of security. They will be attacked when the Antichrist breaks their treaty at the midpoint of the Tribulation, and the battle of Gog and Magog will begin.

The scripture clearly says that at the end of the Battle of Gog and Magog, Israel will believe in the name of the Lord from that day forward and forever (Ezekiel 39:21-22). That could not be true if the battle occurs before the Tribulation Period, because during the Tribulation Period, the Jews will sign a peace treaty with the Antichrist, trusting in him to protect them instead of God. Once Jesus returns, however, and He has rescued Israel by defeating all their enemies at the Battle of Armageddon, they will finally believe only in the name of the Lord, and they will do so for eternity.

I believe that the battle of Gog and Magog will wage for the second half of the Tribulation, and then it will culminate in the battle of Armageddon, when Jesus will put a stop to the fighting. The descriptions of the scavenging birds that will feast on those who die in battle are almost identical in the prophecies about the Battle of Gog and Magog and the Battle of Armageddon—compare Ezekiel 39:17-20 to Revelation 19:17-18. The scriptures about the spoils of each battle being gathered also read very similarly—compare Zechariah 14:14 to Ezekiel 39:10. I believe that the spoils from each battle will be gathered at the same time, for seven years into the Millennial Kingdom. This would create a beautiful symmetry; seven years of chaos, strife, and judgment in the Tribulation will be followed by seven years of bounty and blessing. God is so merciful and loving that even after those seven years of bounty, He will give us 993 more years of peace and blessing that we do not deserve! The Millennial Kingdom is coming, and if you believe in the name of Jesus alone to save

you and be Lord of your life, you will be a part of it! Praise the
Lord for the greatness of His eternal plan.

Chapter Thirteen
The Millennial Kingdom
Revelation 19:6-10, 20:1-10

•••

The Marriage Supper of the Lamb
Revelation 19:6-10

The Bible talks about a literal and physical Millennial Kingdom. The purpose of the Millennial Kingdom is to celebrate the marriage between the Bride of Christ (which at that time will include the Church, the Tribulation saints, and the redeemed of Israel) and Jesus. It will be a physical Kingdom and a thousand-year party celebrating that union. The Marriage Supper of the Lamb will kick off the Millennial Kingdom. In Hebrew tradition, the marriage supper was the last part of the wedding events; it announced the union to everyone in the community. God created the Hebrew marriage tradition to give us a picture of how our redemption as the Bride of Christ works.

The Hebrew marriage ceremony had three distinct parts. The first part was the betrothal. During this phase, the groom purchased his bride, and the groom went away to prepare a home for her while she readied herself for his return. Betrothal was more serious than engagements of today, as it was a binding legal agreement that required divorce to break off (Matthew 1:18-19). Once the preparations of the betrothal period were complete, the groom would return, gather his bride, and take her to a private wedding ceremony. Friends and family did not attend this ceremony; it was just between the bride and groom. After the ceremony, the couple would consummate the marriage. The third and final part of the marriage process was an elaborate marriage supper when all the couple's loved ones would come together to celebrate the marriage.

Our husband-and-wife relationships on earth are a picture of Christ's relationship with the Church (Ephesians 5:25-32). Each stage of the Hebrew marriage process clearly represents a different stage of our relationship with Jesus Christ. Right now, the Bride of Christ is the Church, and we are in the betrothal period. The Bridegroom has purchased and redeemed us, and He has gone to prepare a place for us (John 14:1-3). In the meantime, we are to prepare ourselves for the groom's return (1 Corinthians 6:19-20). We are betrothed to Him, but we have not yet had the ceremony or the marriage supper. We were purchased and redeemed by Jesus' death on the cross. He purchased us with His own blood, and so our response is to cleanse ourselves via the Spirit so that we may be properly presented to Jesus when He returns (2 Corinthians 11:2).

The second phase of a Hebrew marriage, the private wedding ceremony, is a picture of what is coming next for the Bride of Christ. Right now, the Church is anxiously waiting and preparing for the Groom's return. When Jesus returns, He will gather His Bride to Himself and take us away to be with Him. This is the Rapture. Jesus will come back to get us, and we will meet Him in the clouds (1 Thessalonians 4:16-17). When He comes, the believers that have died and are presently living with Him (2 Corinthians 5:6-8) will return with Him and take part in the private marriage ceremony along with us. Jesus will take us all back to the home that He has prepared for us via His death on the cross, and we will become one with Him in heaven.

Finally, the marriage supper traditional to Hebrew marriages is a depiction of the Marriage Supper of the Lamb and the Millennial Kingdom as a whole. Hebrew marriage feasts would last for weeks, only ending when the food ran out.

Food will not run out in the Millennial Kingdom, so the celebration of our marriage with Christ will last for a thousand years! This celebration will finally include the entire Bride of Christ, which will be made up of not only the Church and Tribulation saints, but also the redeemed of Israel. Israel is not a part of the Bride of Christ right now because they have not yet returned to follow God. After the Tribulation is over, Israel will finally be ready to receive the Groom when He returns for her, and they will be married. The Millennial Kingdom will be a celebration of the complete Bride of Christ and our marriage to the Lamb.

God viewed Israel as His wife, but she was unfaithful, so God gave her a certificate of divorce (Jeremiah 3:6-8). Despite the Jews' unfaithfulness, God has promised to gather them back and remarry them (Isaiah 54:4-8). The new covenant that God will make with Israel in the future will reconcile them to Him, and it will never be broken (Jeremiah 31:31-40). We in the Church already participate in this new covenant through Jesus because the promises that God made to Israel are available to the Church now (Ephesians 3:4-6). The Church has not taken the place of Israel. God prophesied extensively about His relationship with Israel. The entire book of Hosea is a picture of that relationship. Israel was unfaithful to God, but God is merciful, and He will buy Israel back. God will yet fulfill more promises to Israel, and He will remarry Israel at the Marriage Supper of the Lamb.

God knew that the Jews would reject the Messiah the first time that He came. The Jews were invited to join the Kingdom first (Romans 1:16, Matthew 22:1-10), and because the Israelites rejected Jesus, He extended His offer of salvation to the Gentiles. We have been invited into God's presence and the Millennial Kingdom because of Israel's unfaithfulness! God is omniscient and merciful, and He knew that Israel's rejection of the Messiah would open the door for many more to join the

Kingdom. God is even more merciful because despite Israel's initial rebellion, He will give them another opportunity to join the Kingdom.

Throughout the Tribulation, God will provide many signs that Jesus is coming back. Jesus exhorted the Israelites to be ready and watching for His return, because if they aren't, they will be left out (Matthew 25:1-13). When Jesus returns, He will judge the Israelites, and only righteous, believing Jews will be able to enter the Millennial Kingdom (Ezekiel 20:33-38). The good news is, all the Jews who endure until the end of the Tribulation will be righteous and allowed to enter the Kingdom. Likewise, only righteous, believing Gentiles will be able to enter the Millennial Kingdom. Jesus will judge the Gentile nations that survive the Tribulation according to how they have treated Israel (Joel 3:1-3). When Jesus sits on His earthly throne, He will give those who were good to Israel righteousness and welcome them into the Kingdom, but those who weren't good to Israel will go to punishment (Matthew 25:31-46).

The Church and Israel are two separate entities (Romans 11:13-18, 24), but at the Marriage Supper of the Lamb, we will become one Bride (Revelation 21:9-14). Israel's redemption is by mercy alone. They, just like us, do not deserve God's mercy, but God gives it to us anyway (Hosea 2:1-23). Israel deserves to be destroyed just like all other wicked nations, but God has promised to redeem them because of His promises to Abraham, Isaac, and Jacob.

God promised Abraham, Isaac, and Jacob that they would receive the land, but they didn't in their lifetime (Hebrews 11:8-10, 13). They were strangers and sojourners in the land of Israel their entire lives, yet God has promised that many will come from east and west and receive God's Kingdom with Abraham, Isaac, and Jacob (Matthew 8:10-11). If there will not be a literal Millennial Kingdom on this earth, then God will never fulfill His promise to give Abraham, Isaac, and Jacob the land. God is not a liar, and He can't break promises. The Millennial Kingdom will be a literal Kingdom on earth, and Abraham, Isaac, and Jacob will be a part of it.

The Millennial Kingdom will be the unmatched celebration of Israel returning to their God (Isaiah 62:1-5). This celebration will be so amazing that when John got a glimpse of it, he fell in worship at the feet of the angel that was showing it to him! The angel had to remind him not to worship anyone other than God. John knew that Jesus is the only one who should be worshipped. He knew better than to worship the angel. He was just so overwhelmed at the sheer majesty of the Kingdom that he couldn't help but worship. The only other thing that caused John to react this way was the sight of the New Heaven and the New Earth (Revelation 22:8-9). This gives us a tiny glimpse into the truth; our current suffering, and even the suffering Tribulation believers will face, is not worth comparing to the glory that is to come (Romans 8:18). Aren't you glad you're invited to that amazing Kingdom, where we will feast and worship for a thousand years?

•••

The Physical Millennial Kingdom
Revelation 20:1-10

The Kingdom of God will come on the earth, and at that time, God's will will be done on earth as it is in heaven (Matthew 6:9-10). God's Kingdom will last forever (Daniel 2:44), but we call the portion of the Kingdom that will exist physically on *this* earth the Millennial or Messianic Kingdom. It can be called the Messianic Kingdom because it is the physical Kingdom of Jesus the Messiah. The Old Testament described many aspects of the physical Kingdom of God, but the book of

Revelation is the first to state how long this Kingdom will last. We call it the "Millennial" Kingdom because it will last for a thousand years. Our passage states that this Kingdom will last for a thousand years six times in just seven verses! God did not make it ambiguous.

Despite the Bible's descriptions of a physical Kingdom of God, many Christians don't believe that there will be a period when Jesus will literally rule and reign on the earth. Those who don't believe in an earthly thousand-year reign usually cite a verse in Psalms (Psalm 50:10). That passage is about how everything belongs to God (Psalm 50:7-12), and in verse ten, it says "the cattle on a thousand hills" as a representation of God's ownership of all land and livestock. They say that since "a thousand hills" is a generalization, we cannot assume that the thousand years in Revelation are literal. This comparison is inaccurate because the contexts of the two passages are quite different. As described above, the context of "a thousand hills" was clearly descriptive of God's complete ownership of the earth. Conversely, if you examine the context of Revelation twenty, it's clear that 'a thousand years' is not hyperbole, because it has clear bounds on it. Satan will be thrown into the pit for a thousand years, but that cannot mean forever, because he will be loosed again. In context, the thousand years describes a set amount of time in which certain things must be accomplished, and so it must be a literal period of time.

Another reason some do not believe in a physical Kingdom of God is because the Kingdom of God is sometimes referred to as the Kingdom of Heaven. This has caused some to believe that the Kingdom of God exists only in heaven. However, there is a remarkably simple reason the Kingdom of God is sometimes called the Kingdom of Heaven. If you look, you will see that the term Kingdom of Heaven is only used in the book of Matthew. The other Gospels use Kingdom of God in the same contexts—compare Matthew 13:31-32 to Mark 4:30-31. The reason Matthew wrote "Kingdom of Heaven" instead of Kingdom of God is because Jews of that time did not speak or write the name of God. They believed it was too sacred to speak or even write. Matthew wanted his audience, the Jews, to understand that Jesus is the Christ, but he didn't want to create an obstacle to their belief, so he called it the Kingdom of Heaven instead of the Kingdom of God. It's as simple as that, but the terminology has still caused confusion. The Kingdom of Heaven and the Kingdom of God are the exact same thing, and the Kingdom of God is a whole lot more than just what happens when we get to heaven.

Many Christians don't believe in a physical Kingdom of God because they know that the Kingdom of God is spiritual, and they just don't realize that it is both. The Kingdom of God has many aspects, and you must believe in all of them to see a true picture of the Kingdom of God. Gene Mims described the complexity of the Kingdom very well:

> The Kingdom of God is the reign of God
> through Christ in the lives of persons as
> evidenced by His activity in, through, and
> around them. The Kingdom was prophesied in
> the Old Testament, pictured in Israel,
> proclaimed by John the Baptist, inaugurated by
> Christ in His public ministry on earth, extended
> in the lives of believers through the Church in
> the present age, and will be consummated by
> Christ when He returns to the earth to rule with
> His saints.[10]

---

[10] Mims, Gene. *Thine Is the Kingdom: The Reign of God in Today's World.* Lifeway Press, 1997, p. 18.

All these aspects are important to remember, because often people think they understand the Kingdom of God when they're only considering one or two parts of it. To have a Biblical understanding of the Kingdom of God, you need to put all of what the scripture says about the Kingdom of God together.

God's physical Kingdom has been prophesied, just like every other kingdom that has ever ruled the world. God's Kingdom has always existed, yet on earth, God has not always exercised the full control that He possesses, and so several earthly kingdoms have arisen to rule the world in their time. Daniel prophesied that God will defeat the last kingdom that will take over the earth (that is, the kingdom of the Antichrist) and give possession of the eternal Kingdom to the saints (Daniel 7:13-27). When God throws down the Antichrist's physical kingdom and gives possession of it to the saints, it will not cease to be a physical kingdom. When Jesus begins to exercise His full authority over the earth and destroys the Antichrist's kingdom, He will give the physical Kingdom to His saints, and He will reign over the whole earth, from earth.

God set Israel apart as a nation of priests that were to be a picture of God's Kingdom on earth. He promised to bless them if they followed His commands, but the nation of Israel didn't come through on their end of the bargain. John the Baptist pleaded with Israel to repent because he knew the Kingdom was at hand (Matthew 3:1-3). The Jews hadn't represented the Kingdom well in the past, but if they had listened to John the Baptist and recognized Jesus as God, they would have been a part of the Kingdom like the Church is now. Since they didn't, God extended the opportunity for salvation to the Gentiles. When Jesus arrived on earth, He brought the Kingdom of God with Him, but the Jews did not believe in Him.

Jesus inaugurated the Kingdom of God in His ministry on the earth (Mark 1:14-15). Jesus praised John's ministry, but He pointed out that being a part of the Kingdom of God makes each of us even greater than John the Baptist, because we get to fully experience the salvation relationship that John only preached about (Matthew 11:11). With salvation comes the Holy Spirit that indwells each of us and directs our every step if we allow Him to. Right now, the Kingdom of God is evidenced on the earth through the lives of believers, since we have made Him our Lord and have His Spirit within us. God's Kingdom exists as the Holy Spirit's activity in, through, and around us.

We are God's Kingdom, yet He is still to come (Revelation 1:4-8). God is not done with His work yet, and so His Kingdom is not yet complete. The Church Age is not the full realization of the Kingdom of God. Part of the Kingdom exists now, but the full image of it will not be consummated until Christ Himself returns to the earth to rule with His saints. After the Tribulation and the rule of the Antichrist, Jesus will defeat Satan and his temporary earthly kingdom, and Jesus will receive His Kingdom forever (Daniel 7:13-14). At that time, Jesus will no longer be called "who is to come" because His Kingdom will be fully realized and consummated (Revelation 11:15-17).

The Kingdom of God is more than just a spiritual thing that exists within us, and it is also more than just a measurable, earthly thing (Luke 17:20-21). The Kingdom of God exists wherever God is King, and God has always been King over the entire universe (Psalm 145:13). The people Jesus taught during His time on earth were too focused on the coming physical kingdom, so they neglected the current spiritual Kingdom. Today, we have the opposite problem. Don't forget that there is a physical Kingdom to come. When the disciples asked if Jesus would restore the Kingdom to Israel soon, Jesus didn't say that He would not physically restore the Kingdom. He simply reminded them that it was not time yet, and the Kingdom existed in a different way at that time (Acts 1:6-8).

God has promised to give the earth to the saints to rule (Revelation 5:9-10, Matthew 5:1-5, Psalm 37:9-11, 22). God started by promising the land of Israel to Abraham, Isaac, and Jacob as an everlasting possession (Genesis 17:1-8; 26:1-3; 28:10-15), and He has grafted us into that promise. The Israelites received the land hundreds of years after God made these promises. By that time, Abraham, Isaac, and Jacob were long dead. None of them received the land in their lifetimes, so that means one of two things. Either God lied, and they will not personally receive the land, or Abraham, Isaac, and Jacob will receive the land in the future. God cannot lie, so they must receive the land in the future. Jesus confirmed that He will fulfill His promise, and Abraham, Isaac, and Jacob will reside in the Kingdom with the rest of the saints (Matthew 8:11). This promise will be physically fulfilled in the Millennial Kingdom, and then eternally in the everlasting Kingdom of God.

All the redeemed of Israel and believers from all nations will be able to live on this earth in that Kingdom to come. There will come a day when Israel will be planted in the land and never uprooted (Amos 9:11-15). What God promised Abraham, Isaac, and Jacob, He will fulfill. Israel still exists because of the promises God made to them (Malachi 3:6-7). If He has been faithful not to destroy them, He will be faithful to give them the land for all eternity (Isaiah 60:21). The Kingdom of God exists now in the lives of those of us who have trusted Jesus as our Savior, but we are just a picture of the full Kingdom that will come to this earth. Believe it!

•••

The Government of the Millennial Kingdom
Revelation 20:1-6

God's structure of government in the Millennial Kingdom will include the Church, Israel, the Old Testament saints, the Tribulation saints, and the twelve Apostles. There will be a Gentile branch of government and a Jewish branch of government in this Kingdom. The Church will rule over Gentile nations, Israel will rule over all the nations of the World, and the twelve Apostles will rule over the twelve tribes of Israel. As this new government is formed, the Old Testament saints and the Tribulation saints will rise again, and God will give them new bodies so that they can take their places in the Kingdom and reign with Jesus.

At the end of the Tribulation Period/beginning of the Millennial Kingdom, the saints will come back to life and reign with Christ for the thousand years of the Millennial Kingdom (Revelation 20:4). At this point, the Church will have already received their new bodies at the Rapture (1 Corinthians 15:50-58, 1 Thessalonians 4:13-18, Romans 8:23), so these resurrected saints must be the Old Testament saints who are with God in spirit, but who have not yet received their new bodies, and the Tribulation saints that will die for the faith (Daniel 12:1-2, 13; Revelation 20:4). Both these groups will receive their new bodies once the Tribulation is over, at the beginning of the Millennial Kingdom, and they will reign with Christ for a thousand years.

The Church will take turns ruling with Christ as the twenty-four elders (Revelation 2:26-27, 4:4). God has been promising that we will reign in the life to come for ages (Revelation 3:20-21, 1 Corinthians 6:1-3). He has told us that we will reign with Christ if we overcome by faith (2 Timothy

2:12). Jesus will rule from Jerusalem and the Church will rule
with Him over the nations (Luke 19:11-19). The Church will
rule over the people who make it through the Tribulation—
those who treat Israel well. During this time, many children will
be born, and people will live a long, long time, but there will
still be sin and death (Isaiah 65:20). Humanity's sin nature will
persist in the people born during the Millennial Kingdom, even
though Satan will be bound. Sin will exist, but it will be
diminished.

In the Kingdom, Israel will rule not only over the Jews,
but also over the Gentile nations, and the twelve Apostles will
then rule over the twelve tribes of Israel (Deuteronomy 15:6,
Matthew 19:27-28). God made promises of blessing to Israel
that have not been fulfilled yet because Israel has gone astray
(Deuteronomy 28:1-6). Those promises will come true when
Israel is finally faithful to God. God has promised that there
will be a day when every Jewish person will have God's Word
written on their hearts (Jeremiah 31:31-34). At the end of the
Tribulation, God will gather the Jews from every corner of the
globe, and they will all know Him (Ezekiel 36:22-27). He will
remove all their iniquity, put His Law on their hearts and His
Spirit within them, and He will move them to follow His
decrees. In God's Millennial Kingdom, all the promises that
God made to Israel about the Promised Land will be fulfilled,
and they will prosper. God will bless them, and by His blessing,
He will show His holiness and faithfulness to all nations.

When God brought Israel into the land the first time,
each of the twelve tribes received an inheritance. The
Reubenites, Gaddites, and the half-tribe of Manasseh received
land east of the Jordan River, and the others received their
inheritance west of the river. The Bible says, however, that the
land will be parceled out differently in the Millennial Kingdom
(Ezekiel 47:13-48:29). Each tribe's boundaries will be different
at that time than they were the first time around (Joshua 15-21).

There will even be a whole new section between Judah and Benjamin for the prince (King David) and the holy ones (Ezekiel 48:8-22). God fulfilled every promise for the first time He gave Israel the land, and likewise He will fulfill all His promises for the time to come (Joshua 21:43-45).

King David will have a prominent place in the Kingdom as God's prince (Jeremiah 30:8-9, Ezekiel 37:22-25). When God gathers Israel back, He will be their Lord and God, but David will be their Prince (Ezekiel 34:22-24). Scripture says this over and over! All these prophecies of David's kingship were written long after David had died. They are not talking about David's first reign. David will physically return to rule from Israel with Jesus. Jesus will rule from Jerusalem, and the city will be the center of worship and power for the entire world. There will be a new temple in Israel during the Millennial Kingdom. We don't know for sure if this temple will be the one used in the Tribulation after being cleansed from the Antichrist's desolation, or a new one that Jesus will build with the nations, but it will be unlike any temple that has yet existed in Israel (Ezekiel 40-47:12). A river will flow from beneath this temple that will create an oasis, even turning the Dead Sea fresh.

The animal world will even be tamed during this time (Ezekiel 34:25-31). God promises that we will be able to sleep in the woods and not get bit by anything, and children will play with cobras without fear (Isaiah 11:6-9). That's more proof that the Kingdom is not fully realized yet! We do not live peacefully with wild animals right now. In the Millennial Kingdom, there will be peace on earth, and we will return to the relationship with animals that we had before the flood (Isaiah 65:18-25). Before the flood, all animals were herbivores, and they did not fear people (Genesis 1:30). When the Millennial Kingdom arrives, we will never be afraid of animals again, and they will not be afraid of us. Everything God has promised will come to pass.

The Millennial Kingdom will be a wonderful place and an unmatched celebration lasting a thousand years. At that time, God will gather Israel back to Himself and remarry her. He will set Israel up to rule over all the nations that once ruled over them. If you are a part of the Church, rejoice that God has grafted us into these promises, and God has a place for you to rule in the Kingdom too. The Kingdom of God exists now in His Spirit's work through the lives of the Church, but at Jesus' second coming He will consummate the full reality of the Kingdom, and it will exist forever, starting with the Millennial Kingdom's thousand-year reign on this earth. It will be incredible, but even still, the best is yet to come! I can't wait to show you what will come next.

Chapter Fourteen
The Final Rebellion and the
Great White Throne Judgment
Revelation 20:7-15

For the thousand years of the Millennial Kingdom, Satan will be bound in the bottomless pit, but when that time is over, he will be released for a little while. He will go throughout the earth and tempt humans living during the Millennial Kingdom. Those who succumb to Satan's temptation will gather one last time to fight against the Lord. After this final rebellion, God will send fire down to consume all the enemies of the Lord, and Satan will be thrown into the Lake of Fire for all eternity. Then every single person who has ever died without accepting God's offer of salvation will rise out of Hades, be judged at the Great White Throne Judgment, and be thrown into the Lake of Fire. They will join Satan, the Antichrist, and the False Prophet in eternal torment.

The Antichrist and the False Prophet are the only two people who will go straight to the Lake of Fire (Revelation 19:19-21). Even Satan will not go straight to the Lake of Fire. He will first be held in the abyss for a thousand years, then when he is released, he will tempt people to rebel against Jesus before being sent permanently to the Lake of Fire. Satan will not get everyone to rebel, but he will succeed in tempting enough people that you won't be able to count the number of the army that will gather against Jesus. Satan won't tempt any of the saints of the Kingdom, whether they are Old Testament, Church, or Tribulation saints; we will be beyond his reach at that time, already in our glorified bodies. Satan will gather the people that he succeeds in tempting for one last battle.

This battle is not the same as the Battle of Armageddon that we studied at the end of the Tribulation Period. The first difference between this battle and the Battle of Armageddon is that for the Battle of Armageddon, Satan, the Antichrist, and the False Prophet will use demons to gather kings to fight against Jesus (Revelation 16:12-16). For this battle, the Antichrist and the False Prophet will have already been thrown into the Lake of Fire, so Satan will be tempting people without them. I do think demons will still help Satan tempt people into joining this battle. It appears that the entire world will be tempted at once, so it would make sense for demons to be involved since Satan cannot be everywhere at once like God can. It is likely that the demons will be bound in the abyss with Satan during the Millennial Kingdom (Luke 8:26-31), and they will be released with him to tempt the whole globe at the end.

Another difference between this battle and the Battle of Armageddon is that those who die in the Battle of Armageddon will be scavenged by birds and buried for seven months (Ezekiel 39:11-20, Revelation 19:17-18). In this battle, the enemies of Israel and God that will come against Jerusalem will be consumed by fire; there will be no bodies left for the birds to eat. God will destroy His enemies even as they gather for battle and so there will be no actual fighting, unlike the Battle of Armageddon. Those who rebel will be consumed by fire, and their souls will be judged and sent to hell.

I mean something specific when I say 'hell.' There are three words in Greek that our English Bibles translate as 'hell.'[11] The first is 'Tartaros.' The Bible only uses that word one time (2 Peter 2:4). The context is about angels who rebelled and were immediately cast into a temporary place of torment until the final judgment, when they will be thrown into the

---

[11] Strong, James. Strong's Exhaustive Concordance of the Bible. Abingdon Press, 1890. Print.

Lake of Fire along with the other fallen angels and everyone else. So 'Tartaros' refers to a place of temporary judgment for fallen angels. The second word translated 'hell' in English is the Greek word 'Hades.' 'Hades' is used thirty-two times in the New Testament (e.g., Matthew 11:20-24, Luke 16:19-24, Revelation 1:17-18, 20:13-14). This 'Hades' refers to a place of fiery torment and temporary holding for those humans who reject God's offer of salvation and die. Wicked humans will be held there until the final judgment, when they will be thrown into the Lake of Fire.

'Tartaros' and 'Hades' both refer to places of temporary holding and judgment for angels and humans respectively. All the unrighteous dead will be judged and enter the Lake of Fire for all eternity. The place called Hades will also be thrown into the Lake of Fire after the last judgment, because the temporary holding place will not be needed any more. Hades is a temporary place of judgment, but all who enter Hades will face the final judgment and be thrown into the Lake of Fire. You cannot be saved from Hades once you're there. There is no such thing as purgatory. The Bible is clear that none may pass from Hades to heaven (Luke 16:19-26). Since the Bible says that you cannot escape Hades, don't let man say you can. When you die, your fate is sealed (Hebrews 9:27). That's why it is so important to respond properly to God's offer of salvation through Christ right now.

When I say that those who rebel will be sent to hell, I mean 'Gehenna,' also translated the Lake of Fire. The New Testament uses this word twelve times (e.g., Matthew 5:21-22, 10:28). This is the ultimate and final hell. It is the place of eternal torment where both the bodies and souls of the wicked will be punished for eternity. The Lake of Fire is a place where the fire never burns out, and the things that it burns never disappear. Satan, the Antichrist, the False Prophet, demons, and every wicked person will eventually be thrown into the

Lake of Fire, where they will burn for eternity, because their souls will never die. Satan is not ruling in hell, and he will not escape judgment. Satan will be tormented in hell for ever and ever along with everyone he tempts. Hell is not Satan's dominion. Satan paces the *earth* in search of someone to devour, and he gives reports to God in heaven of what he has been doing (1 Peter 5:8, Job 1:6-7). Right now, he is still allowed to be in the presence of God, and he spends his time accusing believers day and night (Revelation 12:10). When his time comes, he will be tormented in the Lake of Fire for eternity, just like everyone else who rebels against God. Do not think for a second that Satan rules over hell.

The Lake of Fire, or Gehenna, is the second death (Revelation 20:14). The word 'death' means separation. We are all born 'dead'—separated from God. God sent Jesus so that we would have a way to be connected with God. We are all dead in our trespasses and sins until Jesus redeems us (Ephesians 2:1-10). None of us are righteous before God on our own (Romans 3:10-12). We were dead, but through faith in Jesus, God has made us alive. Those of us who have been born again through faith in Jesus Christ, who have been given righteousness by God and will reign with Him in the Millennial Kingdom, do not have to worry about the second death because we have been brought close to God (John 5:22-29). We were dead once, but we will never spiritually die again because God has made us alive in Him. Our physical bodies may die, but our souls will never die of separation from God (John 11:25-27).

Those who will deal with the second death are born dead in their sins and separate from God just like the rest of us, but unlike the saints, they die physically before connecting to God. They live their whole lives for themselves, rejecting God's offer of salvation, and when they physically die, they go to Hades. At the end of the Millennial Kingdom, when Satan has tempted everyone and God consumes those who decide to come against Jesus, Satan will be thrown into the Lake of Fire to be tormented forever. All the wicked that are in Hades will soon follow him.

The final judgment that will send the residents of Hades to the second death is called the Great White Throne Judgment. John saw the great white throne, and someone seated on it, in his visions. You might think that the figure on the throne is God the Father, but God the Father judges no one. He has handed all judgment over to the Son (John 5:22). Jesus will sit on that great white throne, and He will judge everyone based on whether their name is in the Book of Life. We who are in Christ have our names written permanently in the Book of Life and we will never experience the second death (Revelation 3:5-6, 2:11). Therefore, the only people judged at the Great White Throne Judgment will be all the dead in all of history that never received God's offer of salvation in Jesus Christ. All the wicked dead will be resurrected, brought before the great white throne, and cast into the Lake of Fire when their names are not found in the Book of Life.

All the wicked will go to the Lake of Fire, yet the passage also says that they will be judged according to what they have done. In preparation for this judgment, many books will be opened, and the Book of Life will also be opened. Jesus will judge each sinner according to how much sin they committed during their life. Jesus will then confirm that their name is not in the Book of Life, and they will be cast into the Lake of Fire to receive punishment based on their sins on earth. God is keeping track of what the wicked are doing, and nothing escapes God (Matthew 12:36, Ecclesiastes 12:13-14). They will all go to punishment, but some will be punished more than others.

To be saved from this judgment, your faith must be entirely in Jesus Christ and not at all in what you've done. You cannot put any faith in your good works; the only way to be saved is by grace through faith in Jesus alone. Our salvation is not tied to how good we've been. To do the good works of the Kingdom, we are to believe in the One that God has sent (John 6:28-29). God gave man the Law to show us that we could not keep it, thereby revealing our need for God's mercy, in the form of Jesus Christ coming to earth to live a perfect life, die a sinless death as a sacrifice for the whole world's sins, and rise again to conquer death on our behalf. Jesus' sacrifice makes it possible for you to be washed clean, made sinless in the eyes of God, and therefore be unified with Christ so that you will never face the second death. This is all possible by God's grace, and all you must do is place your faith fully in Jesus Christ and what He has done for you. He is real, He is alive, and He offers the gift of salvation to you. He will erase your sin, put His Spirit within you, and you will never have to experience the second death. Isn't that a wonderful thing?

Chapter Fifteen
The New Heaven and New Earth
Revelation 21:1-22:9

•••

Characteristics of the Eternal State
Revelation 21:1-5

After John's vision of the Millennial Kingdom and the Great White Throne Judgment, he saw a New Heaven and a New Earth. The New Heaven and New Earth is not the same as the Millennial Kingdom! It may help to differentiate the two by calling the New Heaven and the New Earth "the Eternal State," because one of the main differences between these two phases of the Kingdom is how long they will last. The Millennial Kingdom will last for a thousand years on this earth, and then the current heavens and earth will be destroyed to make way for the New Heaven and New Earth. This new creation will be the final phase of God's Kingdom, and it is often called the Eternal State because it will last forever. The Millennial Kingdom will be an improved version of life on earth. The New Heaven and New Earth will be a completely new creation, and the place where God will come to dwell with us for the rest of eternity.

The place that we currently think of as heaven, the place where God resides right now, does not need to be remade because there is no sin in heaven. So, when Revelation describes a 'New Heaven,' it is not referring to the place that God dwells. In the Jewish understanding, there are three heavens, described altogether by the word 'shamayim.' The first heaven is the visible sky where birds fly; the second heaven is space, where the stars hang; and the third heaven beyond that is

Paradise, or the presence of God. That's why when Paul said that he was taken to the third heaven, it was understood that he was taken into God's presence (2 Corinthians 12:2-3). When Revelation describes a 'New Heaven,' it is referring to the first two heavens, what we call sky and space. These must be made new along with the earth because they have all been tainted by sin. The earth will be redeemed and temporarily renewed for the period of the Millennial Kingdom, but the earth must be destroyed and a new one created to truly make all things new (Revelation 21:5).

There will be many physical differences between the Millennial Kingdom and the New Heaven and New Earth. The Millennial Kingdom will exist on this cleansed and renewed earth. When the Millennial Kingdom is over, God will initiate the Eternal State by destroying the current heaven and earth and creating the New Heaven and New Earth. We know that the earth will be new because the scriptures say it, and because the New Heaven and New Earth will not have several defining elements of the current heaven and earth. The seas will continue to exist during the Millennial Kingdom (Ezekiel 47:15-20), but there will be no sea on the New Earth (Revelation 21:1). There will still be water, but giant oceans won't be necessary to function as barriers between nations, because there will be true peace. There will still be heavenly bodies during the Millennial Kingdom (Isaiah 66:22-23), but there will be no sun or moon in the New Heaven and New Earth (Revelation 21:23-25). We will not need the sun and moon because God will give us the light that we need, and it will never be night in the New Heaven and New Earth.

The city of Jerusalem will be different in the Eternal State as well. In the Millennial Kingdom, the circumference of Jerusalem will be about six miles, and there will be a temple in that city (Ezekiel 48:35, 47:1-2). When the New Jerusalem descends from heaven in the New Heaven and New Earth, its circumference will be 5,600 miles (Revelation 21:10-17). That cannot be the same city! The New Jerusalem will be so huge that each of its four walls will be 1,400 miles long and 1,400 miles tall. That is more than five times the distance to the International Space Station! This Jerusalem could not exist on this current earth. After the Millennial Kingdom ends, God will make a New Heaven and New Earth that will be large enough to house God's city, the New Jerusalem. There will be no temple in that city because both God the Father and Jesus will live with us on the New Earth (Revelation 21:22). We will not need a temple to act as a temporary dwelling place for God because He will abide with us permanently!

Last of all, a key difference between the Millennial Kingdom and the New Heaven and New Earth is the fact that in the Millennial Kingdom, there will still be death. The Millennial Kingdom is not heaven; it will be made up of survivors of the Tribulation as well as all the saints. The survivors will marry and have children in the Millennial Kingdom, and they and their children will live a lot longer than people do today, but some will still die (Isaiah 65:18-23). Conversely, the New Heaven and New Earth will be a new creation in which death will be no more, and both God the Father and Jesus will dwell physically with us (Revelation 21:3-4). It is the final form of heaven, and only those who have a personal relationship with Jesus will reside in it. Those who enter the New Heaven and New Earth will have eternal life, hence why it is called the Eternal State. Everyone who enters the paradise of the New Heaven and New Earth will dwell with and worship God forever.

At that time, the dwelling place of God will be *with man*. For years, Christian theology has viewed entering heaven as going to be with God (John 14:1-3). That is how it works now, in the Church Age, but that is not the ultimate definition of eternity. God's vision of eternity is not us coming to be with

Him, but Him coming to be with us. God's long-term, eternal desire is to be with us (Leviticus 26:11-13). Let that sink in! The God of the universe who created us wants nothing more than to physically dwell with us. That should blow your mind! God's desire has always been to be with us (Ezekiel 37:26-28). That's why at this point God says, "*now* the dwelling place of God is with men" (Revelation 21:3). The New Heaven and the New Earth is the final realization of the plan that God has had from the beginning.

In the Garden, God walked and talked with Adam and Eve because there was no sin to hinder their relationship yet. When Adam and Eve sinned, they died spiritually and were kicked out of the Garden, causing humanity to be separated from God from then on. Now, Jesus is the only way that we can be connected to God, but in the New Heaven and New Earth, we will walk and talk with God face to face. Right now, our flesh, the world, and Satan pull us away from God. When we reach the Eternal State, all those things will no longer exist. We will have new bodies, we will live in a New Heaven and New Earth, and Satan will be eternally bound in the Lake of Fire. In the New Heaven and New Earth, nothing and nobody will pull you away from God, and that's why the dwelling place of God can finally be with man.

I cannot wait for the day when God descends to live with us, but there is even better news: we do not have to wait until then to be that close with God! God gave us Jesus to be our Savior and connection to God the Father. The Holy Spirit lives within those who come to faith in Jesus, and He comes to us to bring us life (John 14:15-21). God wants to be with His children now as well as in eternity. Focus on loving God and you will grow closer to Him, and you will naturally obey His commandments (Galatians 5:16). Receive His love, and when you do, you will respond in love. Get up every morning and get to know the God who sent His Son to die for you and wants to be with you.

God told John to "write this down, for these words are trustworthy and true." This doesn't mean that God didn't want the rest of the book written down, or that the rest of the book isn't true. Everything recorded in the Bible is God-breathed and true; there aren't parts of the Bible that are more or less true than any other part (2 Timothy 3:16). God used this phrase to call particular attention to what He said next. He said that it is done; your eternity is paid for. As much as the New Heaven and New Earth is something that is yet future, you can have the guarantee of eternity <u>now</u> by receiving Jesus Christ as your Lord and Savior. Jesus' death on the cross conquered sin and death once and for all, so acknowledge your sin and receive Jesus' forgiveness to begin your eternity now. God doesn't want to wait until the New Heaven and New Earth to be with you.

●●●

Your Place in the Presence of God
Revelation 21:6-27

Jesus made many promises to those who conquer (Revelation 2:7, 11, 26-29; 3:5-6, 12-13, 21-22). Here at the end of Revelation, He makes another promise (21:7). He promises that the conquerors will be His children. I don't know about you, but I want to be counted among the conquerors. So how can we make sure that we will be? We must have faith and stand firm until the end (1 John 5:1-5). Then all God's promises will come true: He will make us pillars in the temple of God. He will give us new names, and He will never blot us out of the Book of Life. If you have faith in Jesus Christ, your heritage is as a child of God, and you will inherit eternal life, including the New Heaven and New Earth.

In addition to His beautiful promises for the conquerors, God added a warning for people who don't pursue God (Revelation 21:8). We who are God's children may have committed some of the sins that are listed in the warning, but the difference is that we have repented and been made new; we have accepted God's forgiveness instead of thinking we can achieve righteousness on our own. We will no longer be judged according to our sins, because of the mercy and grace of Christ Jesus (1 Corinthians 6:9-11). Unfortunately, those whom this warning is directed to will be held accountable for every idle word they say, because they reject God's offer of salvation (Matthew 12:36). Do not reject God. Accept His salvation and be added to the number of conquerors.

When an angel showed John the conquerors, he didn't see a crowd of people. Instead, John saw a city. He saw the New Jerusalem coming down out of the sky. We who are united with God are the Bride of Christ, so why did John see a city and not a people? The simple answer is that a city is made up of people. The conquerors are living stones that make up the Church, built on the cornerstone of Jesus Christ (1 Peter 2:4-10). Not only has God come to indwell us individually, but as He's building His eternal people, Jews and Gentiles together become a temple, a holy dwelling place for the Spirit (Ephesians 2:18-22). The twelve tribes of Israel are inscribed on the New Jerusalem's gates and the twelve Apostles are its pillars. The New Jerusalem will be made up of all the saints, hence why scripture describes the city as the Bride of Christ. When God sees this city, He sees its people.

We've seen that there is a temple in heaven and that conquerors will be pillars in the temple of the New Jerusalem, and yet the Bible also says that there will be no temple in the New Heaven and New Earth (Revelation 3:12-13, 21:22). How can this be? How can there be a temple in heaven (Revelation 7:13-15, 11:19, 15:5-8), and the New Heaven and New Earth is heaven, yet there be no temple in the New Heaven and New Earth? The temple is pictured in heaven because the temple is the presence of God. In the New Heaven and New Earth, God the Father and Jesus will dwell bodily with us. The temple is where God is; it's His presence that creates the temple. God will live and be present in the New Jerusalem, so His presence will make the entire New Jerusalem His temple.

The temple of God on earth was created as a place for God to dwell. When we see descriptions in Revelation of the temple, the throne in the temple, and the Ark of the Covenant in the temple, these are physical objects that represent the presence of God. When God makes the New Jerusalem, there will no longer be need of a physical temple because God Himself will live with us. We will worship Him while He is right there with us. The temple in heaven described in Revelation is just a picture of the role that the New Jerusalem will fulfill. In the New Heaven and New Earth, we will get to be where God is for eternity. Therefore, we will be a part of the temple of God because we will forever be in the presence of God.

God designed the Holy of Holies in Solomon's temple to echo this future city. Just as the Holy of Holies was the sacred dwelling place of God, so will the New Jerusalem be. God designed the Holy of Holies to be a perfect cube representing His perfection, just like the New Jerusalem (1 Kings 6:19-22) The walls of the New Jerusalem will each be 1,400 miles long and tall. The walls will have to be 216 feet thick to support the height of the walls! That's a huge city! Its volume will be 2,744 million cubic miles. That is so big that our minds can't really make sense of the number. To give you an idea, the volume of all the earth's oceans is a mere 322 million cubic miles. That wouldn't even fill up a quarter of the city! The city will need to be that big because it will house all righteous people from throughout history. We will all have plenty of room to live in that perfect city with God.

God has designed this coming city to reflect His perfection. The city will be perfect because of His presence. There will be no need for the sun or the moon because He will be all the light that we need. There will be no more night and no need to shut the gates of the city because fear of attack, wild animals, and all types of evil will be gone. I also believe that the new bodies that God has promised us will be like Jesus' resurrected body (1 John 3:1-2), and the perfection of our new bodies will make us feel right at home in the enormous, perfect New Jerusalem. God has planned a place for each of us in the New Heaven and New Earth. The humbler you are here, the more you will be rewarded with then and there. The more faithful you are to let God work through you in the way He chooses now, the more He will put you in charge of then. The first will be last, and the last will be first. Don't jockey for position here on the earth. Instead, consider your place in perfect eternity.

●●●

Living and Reigning in the Eternal Kingdom
Revelation 22:1-9

Over the years, there has been a misconception that when all the saints reach the eternal state, we will all be the same. However, the Bible doesn't teach that! Different nationalities will continue to exist in the eternal state (Revelation 5:8-10). God created us to be different; it's not something that needs to be changed. God made the nations, and He reaches out to and saves people from all the nations (Revelation 7:9-12). God has a heart for all the different tribes, languages, people, and nations of the world. God planned all the different nations from the beginning (Genesis 17:1-8). He called Abraham the father of all nations because all the nations would eventually be able to join Abraham's spiritual family (Romans 4:16-25). All those who trust God by faith are grafted into the nation of Israel. Therefore, all who come to faith from every nation become children of Abraham. Differences are part of God's design, and they contribute to His glory. When we come together, we get a better picture of who God really is. The scripture teaches us that God will be glorified throughout the nations (Psalm 66:1-7, 46:8-11). Getting rid of differences is counterproductive to God's glory.

In addition to God's Kingdom varying in race, there will still be various levels of authority in the New Heaven and New Earth. There have always been different levels of authority for the angels in heaven, and the Eternal State will be no different. God assigns all authority in heaven and on earth (John 19:10-11). He designed authority and He determines who gets it. He places people in power and removes them from power when it's time. That won't stop when we get to heaven. Many people understand that we will reign in the Millennial Kingdom, but they don't realize that that will continue into the New Heaven and New Earth. In the Millennial Kingdom, we will rule over the world, but in eternity we will rule over angels (1 Corinthians 6:1-3). We who overcome will be coheirs with Christ, and what He receives, we will receive (Romans 8:16-17). He is going to rule and reign for eternity, and so will we. God sits in eternity commanding the angels right now, but at some point, when we are glorified with Jesus, we will become co-heirs and rule and reign with Him. Be lowly in the eyes of the world, and you will rule and reign in eternity.

God the Father and Jesus the Son will reign over the whole New Heaven and New Earth, and their throne will be established in the New Jerusalem. It will be the focal point of the New Jerusalem. The river of life will issue from the throne of God and flow down the streets of gold. The tree of life will be rooted on the banks of the river. This tree is the same one that existed in the Garden of Eden when Adam and Eve chose instead to eat from the tree of the knowledge of good and evil (Genesis 2:8-17, 3:1-6). Because of this choice, Adam and Eve were kicked out of the garden and humanity has not been allowed to eat of the tree of life ever since. In the New Jerusalem, the tree of life will be accessible again, and it will feed everyone in the Kingdom (Revelation 2:7). The Garden of Eden was a picture of the perfection of the New Heaven and New Earth, but it was ruined by sin. Praise God that there will be no more sin in the Eternal State. The tree of life will be rooted on both sides of the river that flows out from the throne, so it will be easily available to everyone. It will produce fruit every month, showing us that there will still be some measure of time in the Eternal State (Revelation 22:2).

The river of life that will flow throughout the New Jerusalem is literal and symbolic at the same time (Psalm 46:4-5). It's an actual river, but it also represents something. The tree of life will also be literal and symbolic because the Bible says its leaves will be used for the healing of the nations, but in the New Heaven and New Earth, healing will no longer be needed because there will be no sickness or death. This tree is not only literal, but also symbolic of God's offer of salvation to all the nations. It is freely available to all, but you must come and partake of it to be healed. The river continually flowing represents salvation in the Holy Spirit (John 7:37-39, Revelation 7:13-17). The Tree of Life represents eternal life through salvation (Revelation 22:14). The leaves of the tree also represent salvation, continuing and renewing forever. All of these will be real things, and I think drinking of the river that issues from God's throne and eating the fruit of this literal tree will serve as a reminder of our need for God, much like the

Lord's Supper does for us now. You are saved, you are being saved, and you will continue to be saved for eternity. For eternity, we will rejoice that we can be with God forever because of His grace alone, and the things that the river and the tree represent.

Nearing the end of the book, John repeats that these things *must* take place (Revelation 22:6-7 repeats Revelation 1:1-3). The prophecy in this book must be taken seriously and literally. The events detailed in this book are not symbolic. They have symbolism and meaning, but they must happen. God is the God of the spirits of the prophets. He told them what to write when they prophesied—not just John, but all the prophets. God designed all the scriptures to point to Jesus (John 5:39). Most of the content of Revelation was already written by the prophets and in the Psalms (Luke 24:44-45). Revelation simply compiles the prophets. Revelation is not separate from the rest of the Bible. To understand it, you must study it in conjunction with the prophets. If the words of the prophets must be fulfilled, the words of Revelation must be fulfilled. Many prophecies about Jesus have already been fulfilled, but there are more prophecies about His second coming than His first, and they must be fulfilled as well. Blessed are those who keep the prophecy of this book by believing and sharing it.

Chapter Sixteen
Keep the Prophecy of This Book
Revelation 22:6-21

If you remember what we learned at the beginning of this book, you'll know that when Revelation uses the word 'soon,' it does not mean that only a short time will pass before Jesus' return. It just means that when He returns, He will return quickly. Jesus repeats over and over in Revelation twenty-two that He will come quickly, and He blesses those who keep the prophecy shared in Revelation.

Jesus commended those who keep the prophecy of Revelation because He knows the human tendency to be lazy. The early Church thought Jesus would be coming back in their lifetime, so some people became lazy. They shirked work because they thought that if Jesus was returning right away, there would be no consequences for their slothfulness. That's why Paul wrote that if a man didn't work, he shouldn't eat (2 Thessalonians 3:10-12). The Church believed in the return of Jesus and was looking for it to happen at any moment, which is commendable, but they let that belief take them to an unbiblical place where they acted as if nothing mattered, and they didn't need to work. Therefore, Jesus made it clear that we are to respect the words of prophecy of this book, and at the same time be responsible with the time that we have.

This book is prophecy. It is not apocalyptic writing; it is not hyperbole or cautionary tales. Our passage emphasizes multiple times that it is prophecy, and prophecy foretells what will happen in the future. The Book of Revelation is not apocalyptic writing. John recorded Revelation during the same general time that the genre of apocalyptic writing was invented, and so it is sometimes incorrectly classified in that way. The genre of apocalyptic writing is characterized by symbolism and analogies, and the scholars that invented the genre claimed that only the enlightened could understand it. The book of Revelation does not belong to that category! It is prophecy (Revelation 22:7).

There are many hints in the scriptures that the prophecy in Revelation is literal and the Kingdom of God will be a physical thing on the earth. Jesus is the God of the spirits of the prophets, so He dictated what they prophesied, and He said that the things listed in Revelation must take place (Revelation 22:6). To make the prophecies clear to the disciples, Jesus interpreted to them all that the Law and the prophets said about Jesus, confirming again that all those things must take place (Luke 24:25-27, Luke 24:44-45). Then He taught His disciples all things regarding the Kingdom, and at the end of that time, they didn't think that the Kingdom was just a spiritual thing. They believed that Jesus was going to physically restore the Kingdom to Israel right then (Acts 1:3-6). After Jesus taught the disciples what the prophets said about the Kingdom, they knew that it was a physical thing.

We know that the prophecies about Jesus' first coming were literal because they came true. The Bible speaks even more about Jesus' second coming than His first, and the prophecies about it are very literal. Just as the prophecies about Jesus' first coming were fulfilled, so must all prophecies about His second coming be fulfilled (Acts 3:18-24). The Book of Revelation is God-breathed, and it reiterates prophecy from the Old Testament. Jesus Himself calls the book of Revelation prophecy, and we must believe Him. I hope that this study has helped you learn how to take Revelation seriously and literally, so that you can read and understand it as prophecy that must be fulfilled. Believe what the Book says. Do not remove things from it and do not add things to it. If you do, God will deal with you seriously.

Since we believe that Revelation is just as true as the rest of the Bible, we must keep the prophecy of this Book. The question is, how do we do that? If you believe that the Bible is true and the prophecy within it is literal and must happen, you have already begun to do it. We must believe the prophecy in order to keep it. Not only that, but we are also to share it. Part of 'keeping prophecy' means passing it on. Don't be afraid to share with people what the Bible says about the things to come. We need to believe that the Word is true, and we need to tell people that it is true. We keep the prophecy of this Book by knowing what it says, believing that the events recorded in it will happen, meditating on it in our hearts, telling others what the Bible says, and getting excited about what is to come. Don't avoid Revelation. Don't avoid studying the end times. The controversies over Revelation can be intimidating, but the beginning of the book contains a blessing for those who read, believe, and keep the prophecy of the book! Study it, share it, and reap the blessing!

John was told not to seal up the prophecy of this book. The time is right for us to study it now. Daniel received similar prophecies, but during his lifetime, he was told to seal them up (Daniel 12:1-4, 8-10). When Daniel was alive, it wasn't yet time for the prophecies to be revealed. They were to be sealed until the time of the end. John was told not to seal the prophecy up because we are now in the last days. In fact, the last days began when Jesus came to earth (Hebrews 1:1-2, 1 Peter 1:20, Hebrews 9:26). The Old Testament prophets searched intensely for the timing of these events when God gave them the prophecies, but they were told that it wouldn't happen in their lifetime. We have the privilege of being on this side of the cross when the prophecies are beginning to make more sense. I admonish preachers and teachers not to forego the teaching of Revelation. God has told us to preach the whole counsel of God, and that includes Revelation (Acts 20:26-27)! If we teach the Bible minus the Book of Revelation, we are not being faithful to teach the entire Word of God. God reveals more to me every time I teach and study Revelation, just as He illuminates the rest of the Bible. I hunger for the words of Revelation just as I do the rest of the Bible, and I hope and pray that studying Revelation literally and chronologically has made you hunger for it too.

We live in a day when many run to and fro throughout the earth and knowledge is increasing (Daniel 12:4). When Paul traveled the world for his missionary journeys, the method of travel was sails and wood. A thousand years later when Columbus went exploring, they were still using sails and wood. Yet in our lifetime, we have seen space shuttles become outdated technology. You have more technology in your cell phone than they had in the first lunar launch, by a long shot. I used to wrestle with and wonder how all the nations of the world would be able to watch the death of the two witnesses at the same time, and now because of television and livestreaming technology, it makes a lot of sense. Many things talked about in the prophecy of Revelation make a lot more sense now (such as Israel being a nation again and Babylon rising as a world power once more).

We are living in an amazing time, and keeping the prophecy becomes more crucial each day. Know it, believe it, share it, and understand that when you do, some people will think you're crazy. That's okay. Tell people what the Bible says honestly and with love. If Jesus takes us tomorrow, I pray that people find and listen to the contents of this study, and I pray that God would use it in their lives. What are you leaving behind? Are you passing the message of Revelation on to your grandchildren so that if they must go through the Tribulation Period, they will remember what you said, and the seed will take root? You cannot know if your family will come to know the Lord in your lifetime, but we do know that they will have opportunities to be saved after Jesus takes us. Leave the message behind for them.

It is a blessing that my close family knows the Lord, but I still want to leave the message behind for others. My wife and I have developed relationships with the people on our street. If our neighbors haven't come to know Jesus before the Rapture, they will wonder where we've gone when Jesus takes us. If they go looking for us because they haven't seen us in a while and the world has gone crazy, they will find a packet on the wall of our house that says, "Are you looking for us?" with a picture of our family. It will inform them that we haven't been taken against our will, as some might say. It will tell them that this is something that we have been looking for for a long time: Jesus has come to take us home. Inside the packet are a lot of scriptures that prophesy what's going to happen after the Rapture. Maybe we'll put a copy of this book in there! We have prepared this packet because we want to be witnesses for Christ even after we're gone. If you'd like to make a packet of your own for people to find after you're gone, visit our website (justapreacherministries.org) to find a downloadable PDF containing the information; all you'll have to do is print it.

Don't seal up the words of the prophecy, share them! Those who reject God's offer of salvation have made their choice, but those who accept God's offer of salvation will continue in righteousness (Revelation 22:11). Both choices lead to your eternity; the question is which eternity you want. Do you want to spend eternity being punished and separated from God, or do you want to spend eternity dwelling with God and worshipping Him? It is not too late to make the right choice. It will be too late when Jesus returns to sit in judgment, so choose Him before that day (Revelation 22:12). Jesus hasn't returned yet because He doesn't want anyone to miss this opportunity (2 Peter 3:9). He implores you to come and drink of the water of life, which is the salvation found in Jesus alone (Revelation 22:17). Come to Jesus before it is too late.

Jesus put this message into His book at the very end. Even after He told us how <u>everything</u> would eventually work out, Jesus' message is still ultimately one of salvation. He wants you to have eternal life in the New Jerusalem. Do not get shut out of the city because of the sin of unbelief (Revelation 22:14-15). Those who reject Jesus will not only be shut out of the city, but they will also be punished in the Lake of Fire for all eternity.

We have been admonished to hasten the coming of the day of God, but the day of His return has already been set (2 Peter 3:11-12 Acts 17:29-31). Do not let anyone tell you that Jesus' return is dependent on what we do. There is a verse in Matthew that some have misinterpreted to mean that Jesus will not return until we preach the Gospel to the whole world (Matthew 24:14). That cannot be true, because if the Gospel has not gone out to the whole world, that means that many have died without receiving an opportunity to be saved (Colossians 1:23). God makes Himself known to every man—no one dies without having an opportunity to receive salvation (Romans 10:18). Matthew 24:14 refers to the angel who will preach the Gospel to the entire world during the second half of the Tribulation (Revelation 14:6-7). We cannot make Jesus' return come any faster, but we can cheer it on, root for it if you will, until it appears. That's how we speed its coming. The day is set; we will not make Jesus return a moment before He has planned to, but God calls us to make way for Him. Come quickly, Lord Jesus (Revelation 22:20)! Jesus is God, and we're not. He has chosen when He is going to return, but it's okay for us to ask Him to come back now! He created everything, and He is the one who will bring things to a close. He is the Alpha and Omega, the beginning and the end (Revelation 22:13, John 1:1-3, Colossians 1:16-18).

Jesus is the bright morning star. He comes to end the darkness (Numbers 24:15-19, Isaiah 60:1-3, Luke 1:67-79). Jesus is the sun, the star that gives light to our days (2 Peter 1:16-19). He has come to us as a gift (Revelation 2:26-29). Right now, because of the Spirit living within us, we have a taste of Jesus' glory. We who have His Spirit within us long for the day when we will be with Jesus forever and fully partake in His glory. Therefore, we say with all the Church, "Amen! Come, Lord Jesus." May the God of grace be with you all.

Bibliography

Harris, Scott L. "Understanding the Vision – Daniel 9:20-27."
Grace Bible Church, Grace Bible Church, 4 Dec. 2011,
gracebibleny.org/understanding_vision_daniel_92027.

Hoehner, Harold W. *Chronological Aspects of the Life of Christ.*
Zondervan, 1981.

Johnson, Jim. "Revelation Study 2015." Justapreacher
Ministries: Revelation Study (2015 - Tuesday Night),
Justapreacher Ministries, 2016,
www.justapreacherministries.org/revelation_study_201
5_tnbs.html.

Kessinger, Tony. *Things That Must Take Place: A Commentary on
Revelation Chapters 4-22.* Tony Kessinger, 2013.

Lewis, Clive S. "Chapter 10: The Return of the Lion." Prince
Caspian, Harper Collins, 1951, pp. 141–141.

MacArthur, John. *The MacArthur Bible Commentary.* Thomas
Nelson, 2005.

Mims, Gene. *Thine Is the Kingdom: The Reign of God in Today's
World.* Lifeway Press, 1997.

Strobel, Lee. *The Case for Christ: A Journalist's Personal Investigation
of the Evidence for Jesus.* Zondervan, 2016.

Strong, James. Strong's Exhaustive Concordance of the Bible.
Abingdon Press, 1890. Print.

We Invite Your Inquiries!

If you are seeking more information on the following topics:
- How to order more copies of this book or Principles of A God-Centered Church
- How to schedule Jim to speak to your church, ministry team or group
- Upcoming Bible Study Cruises

Or if you want to view any of the following materials:
- A downloadable PDF Rapture packet
- Recordings of sermons, Bible studies and devotionals
- The Justapreacher Ministries Newsletter

Or any other information tied to this ministry, please visit the Justapreacher Ministries website:
www.justapreacherministries.org
OR
Email us
jim@justapreacherministries.org
Write to us
Jim Johnson
P.O. Box 372236
Satellite Beach, Florida 32937-4140
Check us out on social media!
Facebook: Justapreacher Ministries/@justpreach
Instagram: @justapreacherministries
Twitter: @justapreacherm1
YouTube: Justapreacher Ministries